Essential Readings in Marketing

Essential Readings in Marketing

Leigh McAlister, Ruth N. Bolton, and Ross Rizley, Editors

MARKETING SCIENCE INSTITUTE

Cambridge, MA 02138 USA

Acknowledgments

The abstracts in this book originally appeared in the *Journal of Marketing* and *Journal of Marketing Research*, published by the American Marketing Association; the *Journal of Consumer Research*, published by the Association for Consumer Research; and *Marketing Science* and *Management Science*, published by The Institute for Operations Research and the Management Sciences (INFORMS). They are reprinted here by permission of these organizations.

Published by Marketing Science Institute
1000 Massachusetts Ave.
Cambridge, Mass. 02138
Design by Laughlin/Winkler, Inc.
Printed in the United States of America
ISBN-13: 978-0-9657114-5-6
ISBN-10: 0-9657114-5-5

About the Editors

Leigh McAlister holds the H.E. Hartfelder/The Southland Corporation Regents Chair for Effective Business Leadership at the University of Texas at Austin. She was Executive Director of the Marketing Science Institute from 2003 to 2005.

Ruth N. Bolton holds the W. P. Carey Chair in Marketing at the W. P. Carey School of Business, Arizona State University. She is currently an Academic Trustee of the Marketing Science Institute.

Ross Rizley is Research Director at the Marketing Science Institute.

About MSI

The Marketing Science Institute connects businesspeople and academic researchers who are committed to advancing the theory and practice of marketing in order to achieve higher levels of business performance. Founded in 1961, MSI currently brings together executives from approximately 65 sponsoring corporations with leading researchers from over 100 universities worldwide.

As a nonprofit institution, MSI financially supports academic research for the development—and practical translation—of leading-edge marketing knowledge on topics of importance to business. Issues of key importance to business performance are identified by the Board of Trustees, which represents MSI corporations and the academic community. MSI supports studies by academics on these issues and disseminates the results through conferences and workshops, as well as through its publications series.

Contents

Introduction: Toward a Common Knowledge Base

Wilkie and Moore, in their 2003 paper "Scholarly Research in Marketing: Exploring the '4 Eras' of Thought Development," point out that the fragmentation of marketing thought is a "powerful, perhaps irresistible force" (p. 141) and that the cost of that fragmentation is that knowledge is being lost.[1] That paper's call to action has stimulated many discussions, conference sessions, journal commentaries, and now, this book.

The purpose of this book is to provide a common knowledge base, one that all factions of the field can share. According to a recent survey of all marketing doctoral programs, there is not even one paper that is read by all marketing doctoral students in all marketing doctoral programs.[2] The paper assigned in the highest number of doctoral programs was common only to 35% of the programs, and less than 1% of the articles were assigned by at least 25% of the schools.

To address this problem, the American Marketing Association (AMA) created a list of suggested readings for doctoral students preparing for their comprehensive exams (available at http://docsig.eci.gsu.edu/). While the AMA list contains many of the articles that were assigned by at least 25% of the schools, even the AMA list covers less than 10% of the full range of articles assigned in doctoral programs. Because the AMA list is designed to prepare students for comprehensive exams, it tends to include a high proportion of survey articles and theoretical frameworks—the tools that a doctoral student needs in order to launch a research career.

In this book, we point to a collection of readings that largely complement the AMA collection. Rather than preparing doctoral students to take comprehensive exams, this book can be thought of as helping doctoral students select a dissertation topic. In addition, the book provides corporate members of the Marketing Science Institute (MSI) and other practitioners with a succinct answer to the question "What do we know about topic x?" To do all this, the book must point to examples of excellent research. Because what comprises excellent research is subjective, we were guided in our selection of articles by the collective wisdom of the field as expressed in the selection of winners of marketing's major research prizes. In particular, this book includes the abstracts of papers that have won one of the following research prizes:[3]

Frank M. Bass Dissertation Paper Award

This award is given to the best marketing paper derived from a Ph.D. thesis and published in an INFORMS-sponsored journal that meets the following eligibility requirements: (1) the paper appeared in an INFORMS journal within the two years preceding the nomination deadline; (2) the paper appeared within five years of the date the thesis was finally approved; (3) when the paper had multiple authors, the Ph.D. recipient made the primary contribution.

Harold H. Maynard Award

This award is bestowed by members of the *Journal of Marketing* editorial review board on an article that has made a significant contribution to marketing theory and thought. The award is sponsored by the American Marketing Association.

John D. C. Little Award

Prior to 2005, this award was given annually to the best marketing paper published in *Marketing Science* or *Management Science*. Eligible papers had to be published in either *Marketing Science* or *Management Science* during the award year. Those published in *Management Science* either had to be handled by the department editor for marketing and use "marketing" as a keyword, or they had to be nominated by their authors. In 2005, papers published in any INFORMS journal became eligible for the award. Prior to 1988, the award was known as the Best Paper Award.

Journal of Consumer Research Best Article Award

This award has been sponsored by the *Journal of Consumer Research* policy board since 1996. Before 1996, the award was sponsored by the Association for Consumer Research. Members of the *Journal of Consumer Research* policy board choose a recipient after receiving nominations from the editorial review board.

Louis W. Stern Award for Best Article on Marketing Channels and Distribution

This award is given to an outstanding article, published in a widely recognized and highly respected refereed journal, that has made a significant contribution to the literature on marketing and channels of distribution. It is sponsored by the American Marketing Association Foundation. To be eligible for consideration, articles must have been published at least three years ago but no more than eight years ago. A panel of three judges selects the winner.

Marketing Science Institute H. Paul Root Award

This award is bestowed by members of the *Journal of Marketing* editorial review board on an article that has made a significant contribution to the advancement of the practice of marketing. It is cosponsored by the American Marketing Association and the Marketing Science Institute. Before 1996, this award was funded by the Alpha Kappa Psi Foundation and was known as the Alpha Kappa Psi Award.

Paul E. Green Award

This award is given to the article published in the *Journal of Marketing Research* in the previous year that shows or demonstrates the most potential to contribute significantly to the practice of marketing research and research in marketing. It is sponsored by the American Marketing Association Foundation.

Robert Ferber Award

The Robert Ferber Award competition is held annually in honor of one of the founders and the second editor of the *Journal of Consumer Research*. It is sponsored by the Association for Consumer Research and the *Journal of Consumer Research*. The Robert Ferber Award is given to the best interdisciplinary dissertation article published in the latest volume of the *Journal of Consumer Research*. (Articles must be submitted for consideration for the award within three years of receipt of degree.)

Sheth Foundation/*Journal of Marketing* Award

The Sheth Foundation/*Journal of Marketing* award is given to articles published in the *Journal of Marketing* that have made long-term contributions to the discipline of marketing. It was established through the generosity of the Sheth Foundation to the American Marketing Association Foundation. To be eligible for consideration, articles must have been published at least five years ago but no more than ten years ago. They are judged on the quality of their contribution to theory and practice, their originality, their technical competence, and their impact on the field of marketing.

William F. O'Dell Award

This award is given to the article appearing five years past in the *Journal of Marketing Research* that has made the most significant, long-term contribution to marketing theory, methodology, and/or practice. It is sponsored by the American Marketing Association.

Because we would like to stimulate work on topics MSI has deemed important, we organize this collection of abstracts according to MSI's 2004–2006 research priorities (available in the booklet "2004–2006 Research Priorities: A Guide to MSI Research Programs and Procedures"). These priorities are the result of a biennial process in which corporate members of the Marketing Science Institute vote to establish the topics on which they want to encourage academic research. Thus, they represent the most pressing business concerns of MSI's member companies.

Recognizing, however, that different groups of MSI corporate members are likely to differ in the orders of priority they give research topics, we have identified four distinct communities of interest among the 2004–2006 research priorities. Members within each community are likely to prioritize research topics similarly.

The Marketing Productivity community, which includes many members from companies with well-known brands, places highest priority on metrics (linking marketing programs to financial performance) and branding (issues related to brands and brand equity). The Customer Management community, which includes an equal number of business-to-business and business-to-customer members, places highest priority on customer management (both channel management and customer relationship management) and growth (new products and innovation).

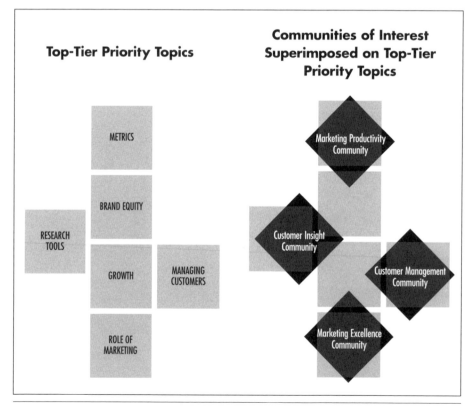

The Marketing Excellence community, which is made up almost exclusively of business-to-business corporate members, places highest priority on understanding growth and the role of marketing. The Customer Insight community, which includes many members with job titles that include the words "research," "insight," or "intelligence," places highest priority on research tools and—not surprising, since customer insight professionals tend to serve other constituencies inside their companies—also on branding and growth.

MSI corporate members also indicated a secondary interest in the topics of marketing mix, customer insight, and strategy. We organize the prize-winning abstracts into nine chapters that correspond to MSI's top-tier and second-tier research priorities. These are:

Top-Tier Research Priorities
- New products, growth, and innovation
- Branding and brand equity
- Metrics linking marketing to financial performance
- Managing customers (CRM and channels)
- Role of marketing
- Research tools

Second-Tier Research Priorities
- Marketing mix
- Customer insight
- Strategy

Each chapter begins with a short summary of the collection of papers whose abstracts are included in that chapter. The directions for future research that follow each chapter summary are taken directly from MSI's 2004–2006 research priorities. These focus on the questions that are most pressing for practicing marketers today. We include at the end of each chapter a list of additional relevant papers whose abstracts can be found in other sections of the book.

This book shows how knowledge accumulates over time and how MSI has influenced knowledge development in marketing. As noted, a number of the prize-winning papers appeared in earlier version as MSI working papers. You will see MSI's influence in research on advertising effectiveness, promotion, service quality, channels, branding and brand equity, the long-term impact of marketing, and the role of marketing in a firm—reflecting the range of MSI's research priorities over the years. The book reveals that core marketing topics are of enduring interest, and that our questions are always being refined.

It is our hope that this book will help to develop a common body of knowledge for the field of marketing, and that by organizing the book around MSI's research priorities, we can focus researchers' energies on marketing practitioners' most pressing problems.

Notes

1. Wilkie, William L., and Elizabeth S. Moore (2003), "Scholarly Research in Marketing: Exploring the '4 Eras' of Thought Development." *Journal of Public Policy and Marketing* 22 (2) (Autumn), 116–46.

2. Bauerly, Ronald J., and Don T. Johnson (2005), "An Evaluation of Journals Used in Doctoral Marketing Programs." *Journal of the Academy of Marketing Science* 33 (3) (Summer), 313–29.

3. Some awards were announced after this book went to press, and are not included in our chapter discussions. The award-winning papers are:

Bronnenberg, Bart, and Carl Mela (2004), "Market Roll-out and Retailer Adoption for New Brands." *Marketing Science* 23 (4) (Fall), 500–18. 2004 John D.C. Little Award.

Cannon, Joseph P., and William D. Perrault Jr. (1999), "Buyer-Seller Relationships in Business Markets." *Journal of Marketing Research* (November) (36), 439–60. 2006 Louis W. Stern Award.

Gupta, Sunil, Donald R. Lehmann, and Jennifer Ames Stuart (2004), "Valuing Customers." *Journal of Marketing Research* (February) (41), 7–18. 2005 Paul E. Green Award.

Hoffman, Donna L., and Thomas P. Novak (1996), "Marketing in Hypermedia Computer-Mediated Environments: Conceptual Foundations." *Journal of Marketing* 60 (3) (July), 50–68. 2005 Sheth Foundation/*Journal of Marketing* Award.

MacInnis, Deborah J., and Gustavo E. de Mello (2005) "The Concept of Hope and Its Relevance to Product Evaluation and Choice," *Journal of Marketing* 69 (1) (January), 1–14. 2005 Harold H. Maynard Award.

Reinartz, Werner J., Jacquelyn S. Thomas, and V. Kumar (2005), "Balancing Acquisition and Retention Resources to Maximize Customer Profitability," *Journal of Marketing* 69 (1) (January), 63–79. 2005 Marketing Science Institute H. Paul Root Award.

New Products, Growth, and Innovation

In this chapter, we cover prize-winning papers on new products, growth, and innovation. The papers are placed into one of five general categories, depending on whether their focus is on

- methods of enhancing new product development processes,
- preproduction testing and evaluation of new product designs,
- methods of forecasting the adoption and growth of new products,
- market entry and defense strategies, or
- contextual and structural drivers of innovation.

Methods of Enhancing New Product Development Processes

Firms face a challenge in deploying the "voice of the customer" in the R&D, engineering, and manufacturing stages of product development. Griffin and Hauser (1993) focused on identifying, structuring, and prioritizing customers' needs, illustrating how a product-development team might use the voice of the customer to create a successful new product. In addition to answering pragmatic questions regarding how to identify customers' needs (e.g., how many customers must be interviewed?), they illustrated how customers' needs can be arrayed into a hierarchy of primary, secondary, and tertiary needs, so that ultimately customers' preferences can be measured and compared.

Shocker and Srinivasan (1979) highlighted the emergence of a new, proactive research mode—multiattribute research—which investigates the structure of customer decisions with respect to the market offerings of a firm and its competitors. They argued that multiattribute research was proactive because its purpose was to develop an understanding of customer decision making sufficient to predict customer behavior in a wide range of future environments, even in the absence of data. More recently, Nowlis and Simonson (1996) investigated the factors that moderate the impact of a new feature on brand choice. They proposed that two simple principles, multiattribute diminishing sensitivity (diminishing sensitivity to new attributes or new features) and performance uncertainty, underlie a wide range of factors that determine the impact of new features. They demonstrated that how new features affect market share and sales volume depends on the preexisting characteristics of the products to which those new features are added.

Preproduction Testing and Evaluation of New Product Designs

New product designs are typically evaluated and tested before the investment necessary for production is made. There is a rich stream of research on techniques for evaluating new products prior to launch, including research on beta testing procedures, pretest market models, prelaunch forecasting methods, information acceleration, and test market methods. Silk and Urban (1978) introduced a set of measurement procedures and models, called ASSESSOR, that was designed to produce estimates of the sales potential of a new packaged good before test marketing, thereby allowing companies to avoid the costs arising from the high failure rate of new packaged goods placed in test markets. Subsequently, Urban and Katz (1983) published a validation of the ASSESSOR model and explored the managerial implications of using it as a predictive tool. Their results suggested that the ASSESSOR pretest market system did well in predicting test market shares. More recently, Urban, Weinberg, and Hauser (1996) showed how a firm could forecast consumer reaction to a really new product by combining managerial judgment with state-of-the-art measurement. Their approach made use of a multimedia virtual-buying environment that simulated future situations and experiences, making it possible to determine whether the new product would be viable at the target launch date, required improvements in technology, or should be scrapped.

Methods of Forecasting the Adoption and Growth of New Products

Since the publication of the Bass model in 1969, extensive research on the modeling of the diffusion of innovations has improved our understanding of the structural, estimation, and conceptual assumptions underlying diffusion models of new product acceptance. Mahajan, Muller, and Bass (1990) provided a detailed review and evaluation of developments in five areas: basic diffusion models, parameter estimation considerations, flexible diffusion models, refinements and extensions, and use of diffusion models. For each of these five areas, they identified a number of research issues that could fruitfully be pursued to help make diffusion models more effective and realistic and more sound theoretically.

Robertson and Gatignon (1986) noted that previous research on diffusion focused on the individual consumer rather than on organizational adoption of innovations. The objective of their work was to introduce an alternative paradigm for research on diffusion, one focused on competitive factors rather than behavioral theory. They proposed an enriched model, based on theories of competitive behavior, for the study of technological diffusion at the organizational level. They offered a set of propositions regarding how the competitive environment on the supply side and in the adopter industry affect diffusion.

Norton and Bass (1987) further enhanced diffusion modeling by examining the dynamic sales behavior of successive generations of high-technology products. New technologies diffuse through a population of potential buyers over time, and diffusion of a new product depends on this demand growth. However, successive generations of a technology compete with earlier ones, a phenomenon that is the subject of models of technological substitution. Building on the 1969 Bass diffusion model, Norton and Bass developed a model that encompassed both diffusion and substitution, and they demonstrated the forecasting properties of their model.

By the end of the 1980s, enough applications of conceptually comparable diffusion models had been reported in the literature to allow Sultan, Farley, and Lehmann (1990) to make empirical generalizations from a meta-analysis of more than 200 sets of parameters from published articles. Their results suggested that the diffusion process is affected more by such factors as word of mouth than by innate innovativeness of consumers, that the coefficient of innovation is fairly stable under a wide variety of conditions, and that the coefficient of imitation varies widely with the type of innovation being examined, the estimation procedure employed, and the presence of other variables (such as marketing mix variables). They used a Bayesian scheme to combine results from the meta-analysis with new data for estimation of parameters in a new situation, a technique that can be especially useful to managers.

Golder and Tellis (1997) added to our understanding of the growth of innovation by highlighting the presence, in the sales growth of many "really new" household consumer durables, of a point of "takeoff" early in the product's history, characterized by a dramatic increase in sales. The takeoff tends to appear as an elbow-shaped discontinuity in the sales curve. They addressed three key questions in their analysis: (1) How much time does a newly introduced product need to reach takeoff? (2) Does the takeoff have any systematic patterns? (3) Can we predict the takeoff? They also showed how a hazard model might be used to predict takeoff, improving managers' understanding of how long it takes a new product to reach takeoff and helping managers distinguish between a large increase in sales and a genuine takeoff.

Market Entry and Defense Strategies

This research stream addresses whether, when, and how a firm should innovate, or alternatively, how it should defend against innovation by competitors. Award-winning papers in this area fall into two categories: those dealing with technological evolution and rivalry and those dealing with rewards to entrants.

Technological Evolution and Rivalry

Research in this area has focused on how best to inform managers about the potential of rival technologies, when such rival technologies will be commercialized, when to quit the existing technology, and when to invest in a rival technology. Cooper (2000) examined how managers could plan responsibly for innovation. He described a framework and method for planning for radically new products and for disruptive or discontinuous innovations that involved mapping webs of the most important factors relating to the new products or innovations into Bayesian networks that could be updated as events unfolded and used to simulate the impact that changes in assumptions underlying the webs would have on the new product or innovation's prospects.

A firm with a good understanding of technological evolution must decide how to exploit that evolution, given the firm's resources and the resources and strategies of its competitors. Ofek and Sarvary (2003) addressed this issue by studying dynamic competition in markets characterized by the introduction of technologically advanced next-generation products. Their analysis suggested that R&D competence can encourage a leader to invest in order to gain technology leadership, while the presence of reputation effects can encourage a leader to underinvest in R&D, leading to alternating leadership between a duopoly of firms.

Rewards to Entrants

Entering a market first may have advantages, and a number of early papers provided support for the notion of market share rewards to pioneers. Theoretical research emerged to explain why and how pioneers might have long-term advantages. In both consumer and industrial markets, a market pioneer might outsell later entrants due to the emergence of a preference structure favoring the pioneer. Such a preference structure might make it difficult for later entrants to "compete away" the pioneer's large market share, even when brands can reposition and switching costs are minimal. Market entry and timing issues are discussed in the chapter on strategy.

Golder and Tellis (1993) reexamined the question of market share rewards to pioneers using an alternative methodology. Earlier studies had been regression based, but Golder and Tellis used a historical analysis that compared mean market shares of pioneers and later entrants. They argued that a historical analysis methodology minimized survival bias and self-report bias. Their study showed that even if there is a pioneering advantage, later entrants are often able to overcome it and (on average) do very well. Consequently, despite the fact that, all else equal, pioneers have an advantage, in actuality pioneers frequently have low market share, mostly fail, and are rarely market leaders.

More-recent studies have developed theoretical models to explain why late market entrants might have advantages over pioneers. Shankar, Carpenter, and Krishnamurthi (1998) showed that an innovative late mover can create a sustainable advantage by enjoying a higher market potential and a higher repeat purchase rate than either the pioneer or a noninnovative late mover, growing faster than the pioneer, slowing the pioneer's diffusion, and reducing the effectiveness of the pioneer's marketing spending. In addition, innovative late movers are advantaged asymmetrically in that their diffusion can hurt the sales of other brands, but their sales are not affected by competitors' diffusion. In contrast, noninnovative late movers have smaller potential markets, lower repeat rates, and less marketing effectiveness than a pioneer.

Contextual and Structural Drivers of Innovation

What are the characteristics of organizations that enhance innovation capability? Does the size of the organization matter? Are small firms better equipped to innovate than large firms? Chandy and Tellis (2000) examined whether new entrants are more likely than incumbents to introduce radical innovation. They found that prior to World War II, small firms and new entrants were indeed more likely to introduce radical innovations. However, that pattern reversed after the war.

Research Priorities

Growth, especially organic growth, is among MSI's first-tier research priorities for 2004–2006. Research topics include the need for better information for decision making (including the question of how to incorporate customer-relevant innovation at all stages of new product or service development), assessment of new product development processes, new tools for proactive understanding of customers, and methods for predicting new product/service adoption. There is also a need for strategic insights into the role of market research in discontinuous innovation and discontinuous growth strategies that reshape an industry.

Abstracts: New Products, Growth, and Innovation

Chandy, Rajesh K., and Gerard J. Tellis
The Incumbent's Curse? Incumbency, Size, and Radical Product Innovation
Journal of Marketing 64 (3) (July 2000), 1–17.
Co-winner of the 2000 Harold H. Maynard Award
An earlier version of this paper appeared as MSI Report No. 00–100.

A common perception in the field of innovation is that large, incumbent firms rarely introduce radical product innovations. Such firms tend to solidify their market positions with relatively incremental innovations. They may even turn away entrepreneurs who come up with radical innovations, though they themselves had such entrepreneurial roots. As a result, radical innovations tend to come from small firms, the outsiders. This thesis, which we term the "incumbent's curse," is commonly accepted in academic and popular accounts of radical innovation. This topic is important, because radical product innovation is an engine of economic growth that has created entire industries and brought down giants while catapulting small firms to market leadership. Yet a review of the literature suggests that the evidence for the incumbent's curse is based on anecdotes and scattered case studies of highly specialized innovations. It is not clear if it applies widely across several product categories. The authors reexamine the incumbent's curse using a historical analysis of a relatively large number of radical innovations in the consumer durables and office products categories. In particular, the authors seek to answer the following questions: (1) How prevalent is this phenomenon? What percentage of radical innovations do incumbents versus nonincumbents introduce? What percentage of radical innovations do small firms versus large firms introduce? (2) Is the phenomenon a curse that invariably afflicts large incumbents in current industries? Is it driven by incumbency or size? and (3) How consistent is the phenomenon? Has the increasing size and complexity of firms over time accentuated it? Does it vary across national boundaries? Results from the study suggest that conventional wisdom about the incumbent's curse may not always be valid.

Cooper, Lee G.

Strategic Marketing Planning for Radically New Products

Journal of Marketing 64 (1) (January 2000), 1–16.

2000 Marketing Science Institute H. Paul Root Award Winner

In this article, the author outlines an approach to marketing planning for radically new products, disruptive or discontinuous innovations that change the dimensionality of the consumer decision. The planning process begins with an extensive situation analysis. The factors identified in the situation analysis are woven into the economic webs surrounding the new product. The webs are mapped into Bayesian networks that can be updated as events unfold and used to simulate the impact that changes in assumptions underlying the web have on the prospects for the new product. The author illustrates this method using a historical case regarding the introduction of videotape recorders by Sony and JVC and a contemporary case of the introduction of electric vehicles. The author provides a complete, numerical example pertaining to a software development project in the Appendix.

Golder, Peter N., and Gerard J. Tellis

Pioneer Advantage: Marketing Logic or Marketing Legend?

Journal of Marketing Research 30 (2) (May 1993), 158–70.

Co-winner of the 1998 William F. O'Dell Award

Several studies have shown that pioneers have long-lived market share advantages and are likely to be market leaders in their product categories. However, that research has potential limitations: the reliance on a few established databases, the exclusion of nonsurvivors, and the use of single-informant self-reports for data collection. The authors of this study use an alternate method, historical analysis, to avoid these limitations. Approximately 500 brands in 50 product categories are analyzed. The results show that almost half of market pioneers fail and their mean market share is much lower than that found in other studies. Also, early market leaders have much greater long-term success and enter an average of 13 years after pioneers.

Golder, Peter N., and Gerard J. Tellis

Will It Ever Fly? Modeling the Takeoff of Really New Consumer Durables

Marketing Science 16 (3) (Summer 1997), 256–70.

Co-winner of the 1997 Frank M. Bass Dissertation Paper Award

An earlier version of this paper appeared as MSI Report No. 97–127.

A consistent pattern observed for really new household consumer durables is a takeoff or dramatic increase in sales early in their history. The takeoff tends to appear as an elbow-shaped discontinuity in the sales curve showing an average sales increase of over 400%. In contrast, most marketing textbooks as well as diffusion models generally depict the growth of new consumer durables as a smooth sales curve. Our discussions with managers indicate that they have little idea about the takeoff and its associated characteristics. Many managers did not even know that most successful new consumer durables had a distinct takeoff. Their sales forecasts tend to show linear growth. Yet, knowledge about the takeoff is crucial for managers to decide whether to maintain, increase, or withdraw support of new products. It is equally important for industry analysts who advise investors and manufacturers of complementary and substitute products. Although previous studies have urged researchers to examine the takeoff, no research has addressed this critical event. While diffusion models are commonly used to study new product sales growth, they do not explicitly consider a new product's takeoff in sales. Indeed, diffusion researchers frequently use data only from the point of takeoff. Therefore, nothing is known about the takeoff or models appropriate for this event. Our study provides the first analysis of the takeoff. In particular, we address three key questions: (i) How much time does a newly introduced product need to take off? (ii) Does the takeoff have any systematic patterns? (iii) Can we predict the takeoff?

We begin our study by developing an operational measure to determine when the takeoff occurs. We found that when the base level of sales is small, a relatively large percentage increase could occur without signaling the takeoff. Conversely, when the base level of sales is large, the takeoff sometimes occurs with a relatively small percentage increase in sales. Therefore, we developed a "threshold for takeoff." This is a plot of percentage sales growth relative to a base level of sales, common across all categories. We define the takeoff as the first year in which an individual category's growth rate relative to base sales crosses this threshold. The threshold measure correctly identifies the takeoff in over 90% of our categories. We model the takeoff with a hazard model because of its advantages for analyzing time-based events. We consider three primary independent variables: price, year of introduction, and market penetration, as well as several control variables. The hazard model fits the pattern of takeoffs very well, with price and market penetration being strong correlates of takeoff.

Our results provide potential generalizations about the time to takeoff and the price reduction, nominal price, and penetration at takeoff. In particular, we found that: (1) On average for 16 post-World War II categories: -the price at takeoff is 63% of the introductory price; -the time to takeoff from introduction is six years; -the penetration at takeoff is 1.7%. (2) The time to takeoff is decreasing for more recent categories. For example, the time to takeoff is 18 years for categories introduced before World War II, but only six years for those introduced after World War II. (3) Many of the products in our sample had a takeoff near three specific price points (in nominal dollars): $1000, $500 and $100.

In addition, we show how the hazard model can be used to predict the takeoff. The model predicts takeoff one year ahead with an expected average error of 1.2 years. It predicts takeoff at a product's introduction with an expected average error of 1.9 years. Even against the simple mean time to takeoff of six years for recent categories, the model's performance represents a tremendous improvement in prediction. It represents an immeasurable improvement in prediction for managers who currently have no idea about how long it takes for a new product to take off. The threshold rule for determining takeoff can be used to distinguish between a large increase in sales and a real takeoff. Some limitations of this study could provide fruitful areas for future research. Our independent variables suffer from endogeneity bias, so alternative variables or methods could address this limitation. Also, the takeoff may be related to additional variables such as relative advantage over substitutes and the presence of complementary products. Finally, examination of sales from takeoff to their leveling off could be done with an integrated model of takeoff and sales growth or with the hazard model we propose. Generalizations about this period of sales growth could also be of tremendous importance to managers of new products.

Griffin, Abbie, and John R. Hauser
The Voice of the Customer

Marketing Science 12 (1) (Winter 1993), 1–27.
1993 John D. C. Little Award Winner and 1994 Frank M. Bass Dissertation Paper Award Winner
An earlier version of this paper appeared as MSI Report No. 92–106.

In recent years, many U.S. and Japanese firms have adopted Quality Function Deployment (QFD). QFD is a total-quality-management process in which the "voice of the customer" is deployed throughout the R&D, engineering, and manufacturing stages of product development. For example, in the first "house" of QFD, customer needs are linked to design attributes thus encouraging the joint consideration of marketing issues and engineering issues. This paper focuses on the "Voice-of-the-Customer" component of QFD, that is, the tasks of identifying customer needs, structuring customer needs, and providing priorities for customer needs. In the identification stage, we address the questions of (1) how many customers need be interviewed, (2) how many analysts need to read the transcripts, (3) how many customer needs do we miss, and (4) are focus groups or one-on-one interviews superior? In the structuring stage the customer needs are arrayed into a hierarchy of primary, secondary, and tertiary needs. We compare group consensus (affinity) charts, a technique which accounts for most industry applications, with a technique based on customer-sort data. In the stage which provides priorities we present new data in which product concepts were created by product-development experts such that each concept stressed the fulfillment of one primary customer need. Customer interest in and preference for these concepts are compared to measured and estimated importances. We also address the question of whether frequency of mention can be used as a surrogate for importance. Finally, we examine the stated goal of QFD, customer satisfaction. Our data demonstrate a self-selection bias in satisfaction measures that are used commonly for QFD and for corporate incentive programs. We close with a brief application to illustrate how a product-development team used the voice of the customer to create a successful new product.

Mahajan, Vijay, Eitan Muller, and Frank M. Bass
New Product Diffusion Models in Marketing: A Review and Directions for Research
Journal of Marketing 54 (1) (January 1990), 1–26.
1990 Harold H. Maynard Award Winner

Since the publication of the Bass model in 1969, research on the modeling of the diffusion of innovations has resulted in a body of literature consisting of several dozen articles, books, and assorted other publications. Attempts have been made to reexamine the structural and conceptual assumptions and estimation issues underlying the diffusion models of new product acceptance. The authors evaluate these developments for the past two decades. They conclude with a research agenda to make diffusion models theoretically more sound and practically more effective and realistic.

Norton, John A., and Frank M. Bass
A Diffusion Theory Model of Adoption and Substitution for Successive Generations of High-Technology Products
Management Science 33 (9) (September 1987), 1069–86.
1987 Best Paper Award Winner (as of 1988, the John D.C. Little Award)

This study deals with the dynamic sales behavior of successive generations of high-technology products. New technologies diffuse through a population of potential buyers over time. Therefore, diffusion theory models are related to this demand growth. Furthermore, successive generations of a technology compete with earlier ones, and that behavior is the subject of models of technological substitution. Building upon the Bass (1969) diffusion model, we develop a model which encompasses both diffusion and substitution. We demonstrate the forecasting properties of the model by estimating parameters over part of the data and projecting shipments for later periods.

Nowlis, Stephen M., and Itamar Simonson
The Effect of New Product Features on Brand Choice
Journal of Marketing Research 33 (1) (February 1996), 36–46.
2001 William F. O'Dell Award Winner

Companies often introduce new product features to differentiate their brands and gain a competitive advantage. The authors investigate factors that moderate the impact of a new feature on brand choice. Building on two principles, multiattribute diminishing sensitivity and performance uncertainty, they propose that the characteristics of the products to which new features are added are important determinants of the impact of these features on sales and market share. Specifically, in six studies, they show that a new feature adds greater value and increases the choice share of a brand more when the brand (1) has relatively inferior existing features, (2) is associated with lower (perceived) quality, (3) has a higher price, and (4) is both high-priced and high-quality. The results also suggest that the addition of a new feature reduces buyers' price sensitivity for low-quality, but not for high-quality, brands and that multiattribute diminishing sensitivity is a more important moderator of the effect of new features than performance uncertainty. The authors discuss the theoretical and practical implications of the findings.

Ofek, Elie, and Miklos Sarvary
R&D, Marketing, and the Success of Next-Generation Products
Marketing Science 22 (3) (Summer 2003), 355–70.
Co-winner of the 2003 John D. C. Little Award and the 2004 Frank M. Bass Dissertation Paper Award

This paper studies dynamic competition in markets characterized by the introduction of technologically advanced next-generation products. Firms invest in new product effort in an attempt to attain industry leadership, thus securing high profits and benefiting from advantages relevant for the success of future product generations. The analysis reveals that when the current leader possesses higher research and development (R&D) competence, it tends to invest more in R&D than rivals and to retain its lead position. The leader's investment exhibits an inverse-U pattern as this advantage increases. In contrast, when the leader enjoys an advantage that originates from the persistence of reputation, it invests less than its followers. Now, followers' investment exhibits an inverse-U pattern as reputation advantage increases. Depending on the extent of leader reputation, industry structure can either exhibit frequent leadership shifts or prolonged incumbent dominance. The basic framework is extended to allow investments in additional marketing variables (e.g., advertising). Interestingly, the leader takes advantage of strong demand for its current product by focusing more on advertising, whereas the follower expends more on R&D. By shedding light on the implications of industry position for investment incentives and market evolution, the analysis provides valuable insights for formulating marketing strategy in fast-paced, high-tech business environments.

Robertson, Thomas S., and Hubert Gatignon
Competitive Effects on Technology Diffusion
Journal of Marketing 50 (3) (July 1986), 1–12.
1986 Harold H. Maynard Award Winner

This article takes as its central concern the diffusion of high technology innovation among business organizations. A set of propositions is developed that focuses on the competitive factors influencing diffusion. The article suggests how the supply-side competitive environment and the adopter industry competitive environment both affect diffusion of new technologies. The article seeks to extend the current behavioral paradigm for studying innovation diffusion by incorporating competitive factors as explanatory variables.

Shankar, Venkatesh, Gregory S. Carpenter, and Lakshman Krishnamurthi
Late Mover Advantage: How Innovative Late Entrants Outsell Pioneers
Journal of Marketing Research 35 (1) (February 1998), 54–70.
1999 Paul E. Green Award Winner

Although pioneers outsell late movers in many markets, in some cases innovative late entry has produced some remarkably successful brands that outsell pioneers. The mechanisms through which innovative late movers outsell pioneers are unclear. To identify these mechanisms, the authors develop a brand-level model in which brand sales are decomposed into trials and repeat purchases. The model captures diffusion and marketing mix effects on brand trials and includes the differential impacts of innovative and noninnovative competitors' diffusion on these effects. The authors develop hypotheses on how the diffusion and marketing mix parameters of the brands differ by market entry strategy (pioneering, innovative late entry, and noninnovative late entry). The authors test these hypotheses using data from 13 brands in two pharmaceutical product categories. The results show that an innovative late mover can create a sustainable advantage by enjoying a higher market potential and a higher repeat purchase rate than either the pioneer or noninnovative late movers, growing faster than the pioneer, slowing the pioneer's diffusion, and reducing the pioneer's marketing spending effectiveness. Innovative late movers are advantaged asymmetrically in that their diffusion can hurt the sales of other brands, but their sales are not affected by competitors' diffusion. In contrast, noninnovative late movers face smaller potential markets, lower repeat rates, and less marketing effectiveness compared with the pioneer.

Shocker, Allan D., and V. Srinivasan
Multiattribute Approaches for Product Concept Evaluation and Generation: A Critical Review
Journal of Marketing Research 16 (2) (May 1979), 159–80.
1984 William F. O'Dell Award Winner

Multiattribute research in marketing seeks an understanding of the structure of customer decisions with respect to the market offerings of a firm and its competitors. Through such understanding the firm tries to evaluate and/or design its offerings for greater customer satisfaction and profitability. Recent applications of such research to new product evaluation and to concept generation are reviewed and critiqued, relevant methodologies are contrasted, and the import of this research thrust for management is assessed.

Silk, Alvin J., and Glen L. Urban
Pre-Test-Market Evaluation of New Packaged Goods: A Model and Measurement Methodology
Journal of Marketing Research 15 (2) (May 1978), 171–91.
1983 William F. O'Dell Award Winner

The substantial failure rate of new packaged goods in test markets has stimulated firms to seek improved methods of pre-test-market evaluation. A set of measurement procedures and models designed to produce estimates of the sales potential of a new packaged good before test marketing is presented. A case application of the system also is discussed.

Sultan, Fareena, John U. Farley, and Donald R. Lehmann
A Meta-Analysis of Applications of Diffusion Models
Journal of Marketing Research 27 (1) (February 1990), 70–7.
1995 William F. O'Dell Award Winner

A meta-analysis of 213 applications of diffusion models from 15 articles relates model parameters to the nature of the innovation, the country under study, model specification, and estimation procedure. The effect of use of the same data by several researchers is examined, as are weighting schemes for improving efficiency of the meta-analysis. A Bayesian scheme is used to combine results from the meta-analysis with new data for estimation of parameters in a new situation.

Urban, Glen L., and Gerald M. Katz
Pre-Test-Market Models: Validation and Managerial Implications
Journal of Marketing Research 20 (3) (August 1983), 221–34.
1988 William F. O'Dell Award Winner

The predictive accuracy of a widely used pre-test-market model (ASSESSOR) is analyzed. The standard deviation between pre-test-market and test-market shares is 1.99 share points before adjustments for achieved awareness, distribution, and sampling and 1.12 share points after adjustment. Sixty-three percent of those products tested passed the pre-test screen and 66% of these were subsequently successful in test market. A Bayesian decision analysis model is formulated and a "typical" case shows a positive value of information. Although some conditions are identified under which a test market may be bypassed, in the authors' opinion both pre-test and test-market procedures should be used in all but exceptional situations.

Urban, Glen L., Bruce D. Weinberg, and John R. Hauser
Premarket Forecasting of Really-New Products
Journal of Marketing 60 (1) (January 1996), 47–60.
1996 Marketing Science Institute H. Paul Root Award Winner

The authors illustrate how a firm can face the challenge of forecasting consumer reaction for a really-new product. For the case of an electric vehicle, the authors describe how one firm combines managerial judgment and state-of-the-art market measurement to determine whether (1) the really-new product would be a viable business venture at its target launch date, (2) the firm should plan for improvements in technology that would reduce price and/or increase benefits enough so that the business venture would be profitable, or (3) the firm should stop development. The new market measurement system combines existing methods with a multimedia virtual-buying environment that conditions respondents for future situations, simulates user experience, and encourages consumers to actively search for information on the product. The authors comment on the advantages and disadvantages of the methodology and summarize the lessons they have learned from this application.

Additional Relevant Papers: New Products, Growth, and Innovation

Alexander, R. S.
The Death and Burial of "Sick" Products
Journal of Marketing 28 (2) (April 1964), 1–7. See page 171 for abstract.
1964 Alpha Kappa Psi Award Winner (as of 1996, the Marketing Science Institute H. Paul Root Award)

Day, George S.
Diagnosing the Product Portfolio
Journal of Marketing 41 (2) (April 1977), 29–38. See page 176 for abstract.
1977 Alpha Kappa Psi Award Winner (as of 1996, the Marketing Science Institute H. Paul Root Award)

Givon, Moshe, and Dan Horsky
Untangling the Effects of Purchase Reinforcement and Advertising Carryover
Marketing Science 9 (2) (Spring 1990), 171–87. See page 121 for abstract.
1990 John D. C. Little Award Winner

Green, Paul E., J. Douglas Carroll, and Stephen M. Goldberg
A General Approach to Product Design Optimization via Conjoint Analysis
Journal of Marketing 45 (3) (Summer 1981), 17–37. See page 94 for abstract.
Co-winner of the 1981 Alpha Kappa Psi Award (as of 1996, the Marketing Science Institute H. Paul Root Award)

Heilman, Carrie M., Douglas Bowman, and Gordon P. Wright
The Evolution of Brand Preferences and Choice Behaviors of Consumers New to a Market
Journal of Marketing Research 37 (2) (May 2000), 139–55. See page 122 for abstract.
2001 Paul E. Green Award Winner

Johnson, Richard M.
Trade-off Analysis of Consumer Values
Journal of Marketing Research 11 (2) (May 1974), 121–7. See page 97 for abstract.
Co-winner of the 1979 William F. O'Dell Award

Lodish, Leonard M., Magid Abraham, Stuart Kalmenson, Jeanne Livelsberger, Beth Lubetkin, Bruce Richardson, and Mary Ellen Stevens

How T.V. Advertising Works: A Meta-Analysis of 389 Real World Split Cable T.V. Advertising Experiments

Journal of Marketing Research 32 (2) (May 1995), 125–39. See page 124 for abstract.

2000 William F. O'Dell Award Winner and 1996 Paul E. Green Award Winner

Ofek, Elie, and V. Srinivasan

How Much Does the Market Value an Improvement in a Product Attribute?

Marketing Science 21 (4) (Autumn 2002), 398–411. See page 128 for abstract.

2002 John D. C. Little Award Winner

Raju, Jagmohan S., Raj Sethuraman, and Sanjay K. Dhar

The Introduction and Performance of Store Brands

Management Science 41 (6) (June 1995), 957–78. See page 31 for abstract.

Co-winner of the 1995 John D. C. Little Award

Roberts, John H., and James M. Lattin

Development and Testing of a Model Consideration Set Composition

Journal of Marketing Research 28 (4) (November 1991), 429–40. See page 131 for abstract.

1996 William F. O'Dell Award Winner

Wensley, Robin

Strategic Marketing: Betas, Boxes, or Basics

Journal of Marketing 45 (3) (Summer 1981), 173–82. See page 187 for abstract.

Co-winner of the 1981 Alpha Kappa Psi Award (as of 1996, the Marketing Science Institute H. Paul Root Award)

2

Branding and Brand Equity

Prize-winning papers on branding cover brand management and brand valuation. The first two papers discussed below provide frameworks for brand management that conceptualize brands as phenomena that are developed through marketing actions. The next two papers provide less conventional brand management frameworks: one focuses on the consumer-brand relationship; one focuses on the consumer-brand-consumer relationships in brand communities. Two additional prize-winning papers consider the halo effect of global brand evaluations on attribute ratings: one delves into the causes of this bias; the other presents a methodology for removing it. The final two prize-winning papers consider store brands and a financial measure of brand equity.

Brand Development Through Marketing Actions
Park, Jaworski, and MacInnis (1986) emphasized the fact that brands are long-term investments that need to be developed and nurtured. They argued for starting with the selection of a general brand image and then elaborating and fortifying that brand image over time. Keller (1993) synthesized the literature related to consumers' knowledge of brands. He defined customer-based brand equity as the differential effect that knowledge about the brand has on customer response to the marketing of that brand. His framework suggested that brand marketing activities should be designed to enhance brand awareness or to improve the favorability, strength, or uniqueness of brand associations, or both.

Other Brand Management Frameworks
Taking a completely different perspective, Fournier (1998) explored the relationships between consumers and their brands. She argued that by conceptualizing the

strength of the brand-consumer bond as brand relationship quality rather than as brand loyalty, marketers gain more insight into the ways strong bonds are created, stabilized, and maintained over time. Further, this conceptualization enriches the notion of brand personality by seeing both the consumer and the brand as active partners engaged in relational give and take. Muniz and O'Guinn (2001) moved from the consumer-brand dyad to the consumer-brand-consumer triad to understand the relationship between brand community and brand equity. They maintained that brands are social entities, created as much by consumers as by marketers.

The Brand-Quality Halo Effect

Van Osselaer and Alba (2000) argued that when consumers learn general brand-quality associations before learning about specific product ingredients or features, the initially learned associations may keep them from recognizing the importance of those ingredients or features as drivers of product quality. Consequently, consumers may overvalue brands and undervalue the ingredients and features that actually drive product quality. Dillon et al. (2001) presented a methodology for removing the bias that such a process might cause in brand ratings. They separated the influence that global brand evaluations and specific attribute cues have on brand ratings, thereby allowing marketers to assess the true strength and uniqueness of brand associations.

Store Brands

Raju, Sethuraman, and Dhar (1995) used data from 426 grocery product categories to validate their prediction that the introduction of a store brand will help the retailer if cross-price sensitivity among national brands is low and cross-price sensitivity between national brands and the store brand is high.

Revenue Premium as a Measure of Brand Equity

Ailawadi, Lehmann, and Neslin (2003) showed that as a measure of brand equity, revenue premium is stable over time and correlates with brand and category characteristics as well as with other measures of brand equity. They pointed out that revenue premium is easy to calculate with readily available data and that it can be monitored through time. Importantly, they noted that it is a single, objective number that both senior management and the financial community find credible.

Research Priorities

Building on these prize-winning papers, MSI's corporate members indicate a continuing interest in brand management. How should brand equity be managed through the product life cycle and for different constituencies (consumers, distributors, press, analysts, etc.)? What is the best brand architecture: a single corporate brand or a collection of independent brands? How do brand personality dimensions affect brand equity for different objectives (trial, preference, loyalty, etc.) and for different product categories? How should consumers' relationships with brands and brand communities be managed?

MSI's members also want to know the best way to measure brand equity, and they want to understand the relationship between brand equity and customer equity, the role of branding in a sales-driven culture, and the impact of brands on organizational effectiveness and employee retention.

Abstracts: Branding and Brand Equity

Ailawadi, Kusum L., Donald R. Lehmann, and Scott A. Neslin

Revenue Premium as an Outcome Measure of Brand Equity

Journal of Marketing 67 (4) (October 2003), 1–17.
2003 Harold H. Maynard Award Winner
An earlier version of this paper appeared as MSI Report No. 02–102, "A Product-Market-Based Measure of Brand Equity."

The authors propose that the revenue premium a brand generates compared with that of a private label product is a simple, objective, and managerially useful product-market measure of brand equity. The authors provide the conceptual basis for the measure, compute it for brands in several packaged goods categories, and test its validity. The empirical analysis shows that the measure is reliable and reflects real changes in brand health over time. It correlates well with other equity measures, and the measure's association with a brand's advertising and promotion activity, price sensitivity, and perceived category risk is consistent with theory.

Dillon, William R., Thomas J. Madden, Amna Kirmani, and Soumen Mukherjee

Understanding What's in a Brand Rating: A Model for Assessing Brand and Attribute Effects and Their Relationship to Brand Equity

Journal of Marketing Research 38 (4) (November 2001), 415–29.
2002 Paul E. Green Award Winner

Although brand ratings capture the favorability of brand associations, they often do not enable marketing managers to disentangle brand-specific associations from other effects. In this article, the authors present a decompositional model for analyzing brand ratings that addresses this nagging problem and provide insights for understanding the sources of brand equity. Starting with consumers' perceived level of a brand on an attribute, the authors decompose the rating into two components: brand-specific associations and general brand impressions. Brand-specific associations refer to features, attributes, or benefits that consumers link to a brand and that differentiate it from the competition. General brand impressions refer to general impressions about the brand that are based on a more holistic view of the brand. In this article, the authors focus on two principal issues: (1) How can the sources of bias that may be present in brand ratings be disentangled? And (2) Do these putatively biasing effects, if present, have any managerial implications for brand equity? The authors demonstrate the properties and advantages of the model in the context of three empirical applications.

Fournier, Susan
Consumers and Their Brands: Developing Relationship Theory in Consumer Research
Journal of Consumer Research 24 (4) (March 1998), 343–73.
2001 *Journal of Consumer Research* Best Article Award Winner

Although the relationship metaphor dominates contemporary marketing thought and practice, surprisingly little empirical work has been conducted on relational phenomena in the consumer products domain, particularly at the level of the brand. In this article, the author: (1) argues for the validity of the relationship proposition in the consumer-brand context, including a debate as to the legitimacy of the brand as an active relationship partner and empirical support for the phenomenological significance of consumer-brand bonds; (2) provides a framework for characterizing and better understanding the types of relationships consumers form with brands; and (3) inducts from the data the concept of brand relationship quality, a diagnostic tool for conceptualizing and evaluating relationship strength. Three in-depth case studies inform this agenda, their interpretation guided by an integrative review of the literature on person-to-person relationships. Insights offered through application of inducted concepts to two relevant research domains—brand loyalty and brand personality—are advanced in closing. The exercise is intended to urge fellow researchers to refine, test, and augment the working hypotheses suggested herein and to progress toward these goals with confidence in the validity of the relationship premise at the level of consumers' lived experiences with their brands.

Keller, Kevin Lane

Conceptualizing, Measuring, and Managing Customer-Based Brand Equity

Journal of Marketing 57 (1) (January 1993), 1–22.

1993 Harold H. Maynard Award Winner and 2002 Sheth Foundation/*Journal of Marketing* Award Winner

An earlier version of this paper appeared as MSI Report No. 91–123.

The author presents a conceptual model of brand equity from the perspective of the individual consumer. Customer-based brand equity is defined as the differential effect of brand knowledge on consumer response to the marketing of the brand. A brand is said to have positive (negative) customer-based brand equity when consumers react more (less) favorably to an element of the marketing mix for the brand than they do to the same marketing mix element when it is attributed to a fictitiously named or unnamed version of the product or service. Brand knowledge is conceptualized according to an associative network memory model in terms of two components, brand awareness and brand image (i.e., a set of brand associations). Customer-based brand equity occurs when the consumer is familiar with the brand and holds some favorable, strong, and unique brand associations in memory. Issues in building, measuring, and managing customer-based brand equity are discussed, as well as areas for future research.

Muniz, Albert M., Jr., and Thomas C. O'Guinn

Brand Community

Journal of Consumer Research 27 (4) (March 2001), 412–31.

2004 *Journal of Consumer Research* Best Article Award Winner

This article introduces the idea of brand community. A brand community is a specialized, non-geographically bound community, based on a structured set of social relations among admirers of a brand. Grounded in both classic and contemporary sociology and consumer behavior, this article uses ethnographic and computer-mediated environment data to explore the characteristics, processes, and particularities of three brand communities (those centered on Ford Bronco, Macintosh, and Saab). These brand communities exhibit three traditional markers of community: shared consciousness, rituals and traditions, and a sense of moral responsibility. The commercial and mass-mediated ethos in which these communities are situated affects their character and structure and gives rise to their particularities. Implications for branding, sociological theories of community, and consumer behavior are offered.

Park, C. Whan, Bernard J. Jaworski, and Deborah J. MacInnis

Strategic Brand Concept-Image Management

Journal of Marketing 50 (4) (October 1986), 135–45.

1986 Alpha Kappa Psi Award Winner (as of 1996, the Marketing Science Institute H. Paul Root Award)

Conveying a brand image to a target market is a fundamental marketing activity. The authors present a normative framework, termed brand concept management (BCM), for selecting, implementing, and controlling a brand image over time. The framework consists of a sequential process of selecting, introducing, elaborating, and fortifying a brand concept. The concept guides positioning strategies, and hence the brand image, at each of these stages. The method for maintaining this concept-image linkage depends on whether the brand concept is functional, symbolic, or experiential. Maintaining this linkage should significantly enhance the brand's market performance.

Raju, Jagmohan S., Raj Sethuraman, and Sanjay K. Dhar

The Introduction and Performance of Store Brands

Management Science 41 (6) (June 1995), 957–78.

Co-winner of the 1995 John D. C. Little Award

We present an analytical framework for understanding what makes a product category more conducive for store brand introduction. We also investigate market characteristics that help explain differences in store brand market share across product categories. Our findings suggest that the introduction of a store brand is likely to increase retailer's profits in a product category if the cross-price sensitivity among national brands is low and the cross-price sensitivity between the national brands and the store brand is high. Our model predicts that the store brand share would also be greater under these conditions. In addition, we find that the introduction of a store brand is more likely to lead to an increase in category profits if the category consists of a large number of national brands—even though the store brand market share is expected to be lower when there are a large number of national brands. We compare the key predictions of our model with data on 426 grocery product categories. The data are consistent with the predictions of the model.

van Osselaer, Stijn M. J., and Joseph W. Alba
Consumer Learning and Brand Equity
Journal of Consumer Research 27 (1) (June 2000), 1–16.
Co-winner of the 2001 Robert Ferber Award

A series of experiments illustrates a learning process that enhances brand equity at the expense of quality-determining attributes. When the relationship between brand name and product quality is learned prior to the relationship between product attributes and quality, inhibition of the latter may occur. The phenomenon is shown to be robust, but its influence appears sensitive to contextual variations in the learning environment. Tests of process are inconsistent with attentional explanations and popular models of causal reasoning, but they are supportive of associative learning models that portray learners as inherently forward looking.

Additional Relevant Papers: Branding and Brand Equity

Carpenter, Gregory S., Rashi Glazer, and Kent Nakamoto
Meaningful Brands from Meaningless Differentiation: The Dependence on Irrelevant Attributes
Journal of Marketing Research 31 (3) (August 1994), 339–50. See page 119 for abstract.
1999 William F. O'Dell Award Winner

Dekimpe, Marnik G., and Dominique M. Hanssens
The Persistence of Marketing Effects on Sales
Marketing Science 14 (1) (Winter 1995), 1–21. See page 39 for abstract.
Co-winner of the 1995 John D. C. Little Award

Heilman, Carrie M., Douglas Bowman, and Gordon P. Wright
The Evolution of Brand Preferences and Choice Behaviors of Consumers New to a Market
Journal of Marketing Research 37 (2) (May 2000), 139–55. See page 122 for abstract.
2001 Paul E. Green Award Winner

Lynch, John G., Jr., Howard Marmorstein, and Michael F. Weigold
Choices from Sets Including Remembered Brands: Use of Recalled Attributes and Prior Overall Evaluations
Journal of Consumer Research 15 (2) (September 1988), 169–84. See page 155 for abstract.
1991 Association for Consumer Research Best Article Award Winner (as of 1996, the *Journal of Consumer Research* Best Article Award)

Mela, Carl F., Sunil Gupta, and Donald R. Lehmann

The Long-Term Impact of Promotion and Advertising on Consumer Brand Choice

Journal of Marketing Research 34 (2) (May 1997), 248–61. See page 41 for abstract.

1998 Paul E. Green Award Winner and 2002 William F. O'Dell Award Winner

Nowlis, Stephen M., and Itamar Simonson

The Effect of New Product Features on Brand Choice

Journal of Marketing Research 33 (1) (February 1996), 36–46. See page 18 for abstract.

2001 William F. O'Dell Award Winner

Raju, Jagmohan S., V. Srinivasan, and Rajiv Lal

The Effects of Brand Loyalty on Competitive Price Promotional Strategies

Management Science 36 (3) (March 1990), 276–304. See page 130 for abstract.

1991 Frank M. Bass Dissertation Paper Award Winner

Srivastava, Rajendra K., Tasadduq A. Shervani, and Liam Fahey

Market-Based Assets and Shareholder Value: A Framework for Analysis

Journal of Marketing 62 (1) (January 1998), 2–18. See page 45 for abstract.

1998 Harold H. Maynard Award Winner and 1998 Marketing Science Institute H. Paul Root Award Winner

3

Metrics Linking Marketing to Financial Performance

Traditionally, marketers concentrated their attention on customer or product-market results, such as awareness, attitude, sales, market share, brand equity, and customer satisfaction. They focused on the short-term effects of marketing variables, rather than long-term effects, and they rarely considered the link to financial outcomes and stock price. However, changes in the business environment have led to an increased emphasis on financial accountability for expenditures. Reflecting this shift, the Marketing Science Institute has designated metrics, or marketing productivity—that is, the measurement of the impact of marketing on financial outcomes—a first-tier priority for the past six years.

Early Beginnings

Marketers have always recognized that marketing variables have long-term financial consequences. In an early award-winning paper, Dean (1966) asked whether advertising belonged in the capital budget. He argued that viewing promotion as an investment could result in dramatic changes in decision making, market testing, measurement, and judgments of how much to spend. Subsequently, Webster, Largay, and Stickney (1980) showed how financial accounting requirements have implications for marketing decisions regarding new production introductions, pricing, and the valuation of individual customers and market segments.

Investigations Focused on Market Share and Sales

The PIMS (Profit Impact of Marketing Strategy) database enabled numerous investigations of the link between marketing variables and profitability. Jacobson and Aaker (1985) used the PIMS database to tackle the question "Is Market Share All That It's Cracked Up to Be?" In their award-winning paper, they reported that the direct effect of market share on ROI was smaller than expected and suggested that marketers should return to fundamentals to determine additional antecedents of ROI.

Long-Term Effects on Brand and Category Sales

At the same time, researchers worked to estimate the long-term effects of marketing variables. (Some of these efforts are covered in Chapter 7, "Marketing Mix.") Dekimpe and Hanssens (1995, 1999) estimated the long-term effect of marketing activity (specifically, media spending) on sales using persistence modeling based on time-series observations of sales and marketing expenditures. The total or long-term advertising effect comes about as a combination of consumer response, competitive reaction, and firm decision rules effects. Dekimpe and Hanssens showed that an advertising medium with lower short-term impact can have a higher long-term effect. Thus, traditional approaches can underestimate the long-term effectiveness of marketing.

Instead of examining brand sales, Nijs et al. (2001) used multivariate time-series analysis to investigate the conditions under which price promotions expand short-term and long-term category sales. They conducted a large-scale empirical study of the effects of prices, promotions, advertising, distribution, and new product activity on national sales of 560 perishable and nonperishable consumer product categories in Dutch supermarkets over a four-year period. Their study allowed them to make empirical generalizations about how marketing intensity and competition influence the short-term and long-term effects of marketing variables. For example, they found category demand to be (typically) stationary around a fixed mean or deterministic trend, with any price promotion effects dissipating within 10 weeks. Higher levels of nonprice advertising, more new product introductions, and competitive intensity reduced price promotion effects. They concluded that price promotions primarily preserve the status quo.

Another way to assess the long-term effects of marketing variables is to study individual consumers' brand choice behavior over time. Mela, Gupta, and Lehmann (1997) studied eight years of panel data for a frequently purchased packaged good and assessed the quarterly effects of price, promotion, and advertising, as well as their long-term effects (i.e., over an infinite horizon). Their results suggest that consumers become more price and promotion sensitive over time because of reduced advertising and increased promotions.

Conceptual Foundations for Considering Financial Returns

More than a decade after the PIMS effort, marketers' attention shifted from market share and sales to more sophisticated financial outcomes. Srivastava, Shervani, and Fahey (1998) developed a conceptual framework that proposed that marketing's task is to develop and manage market-based assets (defined as assets arising from the firm's interactions with its environment), such as customer, channel, and partner relationships. They argued that such market-based assets increase shareholder value by accelerating and enhancing cash flows, lowering the volatility and vulnerability of cash flows, and increasing the residual (long-run annuity) value of cash flows. Their paper stimulated additional work on this topic, including several papers published in an MSI-sponsored special section of the October 2004 issue of the *Journal of Marketing* entitled "Linking Marketing to Financial Performance and Firm Value."

Financial Returns on Marketing Expenditures

Between 1995 and 2004, Rust and his colleagues published a series of award-winning papers that showed how marketing expenditures could be evaluated in terms of their financial returns. Initially, Rust, Zahorik, and Keiningham (1995) provided a managerial framework for assessing investments in service quality improvement efforts. Then, Rust, Moorman, and Dickson (2002) tackled the question of whether financial benefits from quality are derived from revenue expansion, cost reduction, or both. Their empirical study, based on managers' reports of firm performance and longitudinal secondary data on firm profitability and stock returns, showed that firms that adopt primarily a revenue expansion emphasis perform better than firms that try to emphasize cost reduction or both.

Most recently, Rust, Lemon, and Zeithaml (2004) extended this stream of research by presenting a unified strategic framework for evaluating competing marketing strategy options in terms of project financial returns, operationalized as the change in a firm's customer equity relative to the incremental expenditure necessary to produce the change. The change in the firm's customer equity is the change in its current and future customers' lifetime values, summed across all customers in the industry. Each customer's lifetime value is calculated from the frequency of category purchases, the average quantity of purchase, and (notably) a brand-switching matrix estimated from either longitudinal or cross-sectional data.

The authors provide a detailed example of how investments can be evaluated using data from the airline industry.

Research Priorities

There has been substantial progress in tackling research questions regarding metrics, but empirical research has been hampered by difficulties in obtaining financial measures (e.g., costs and profitability). MSI's current research priorities include the following first-tier priorities:

- assessing the impact of marketing programs on financial metrics
- using ROI to allocate resources across function, marketing vehicles, and geographies over time
- valuing intangible assets, such as brand equity and customer equity, and relating them to each other
- linking intermediate marketing program outcomes (e.g., awareness) to financial metrics
- assessing moderating effects, such as advertising's effects on sales, price premium, sales call effectiveness, and distribution

Abstracts: Metrics Linking Marketing to Financial Performance

Dean, Joel

Does Advertising Belong in the Capital Budget?

Journal of Marketing 30 (4) (October 1966), 15–21.

1966 Alpha Kappa Psi Award Winner (as of 1996, the Marketing Science Institute H. Paul Root Award)

Whether advertising is an investment and so should be treated like other parts of the capital budget is a question of moment to marketing managers. Viewing promotion as an investment could bring dramatic changes in decision-making, market-testing, measurements of effectiveness, and value judgments that are required in determining how much to spend on promotion. The economic case for an investment approach to the advertising budget is the theme of this article by a distinguished economist.

Dekimpe, Marnik G., and Dominique M. Hanssens

The Persistence of Marketing Effects on Sales

Marketing Science 14 (1) (Winter 1995), 1–21.

Co-winner of the 1995 John D. C. Little Award

Are marketing efforts able to affect long-term trends in sales or other performance measures? Answering this question is essential for the creation of marketing strategies that deliver a sustainable competitive advantage. This paper introduces persistence modeling to derive long-term marketing effectiveness from time-series observations on sales and marketing expenditures. First, we use unit-root tests to determine whether sales are stable or evolving (trending) over time. If they are evolving, we examine how strong this evolution is (univariate persistence) and to what extent it can be related to marketing activity (multivariate persistence). An empirical example of sales and media spending for a chain of home-improvement stores reveals that some, but not all, advertising has strong trend-setting effects on sales. We argue that traditional modeling approaches would not pick up these effects and, therefore, seriously underestimate the long-term effectiveness of advertising. The paper concludes with an agenda for future empirical research on long-run marketing effectiveness.

Dekimpe, Marnik G., and Dominique M. Hanssens
Sustained Spending and Persistent Response: A New Look at Long-Term Marketing Profitability
Journal of Marketing Research 36 (4) (November 1999), 397–412.
2000 Paul E. Green Award Winner
An earlier version of this paper appeared as MSI Report No. 97–102.

An intuitively appealing decision rule is to allocate a company's scarce marketing resources to where they have the greatest long-term benefit. This principle, however, is easier to accept than it is to execute, because long-run effects of marketing spending are difficult to estimate. The authors address this problem by examining the behavior of market response and marketing spending over time and identify four common strategic scenarios: business as usual, hysteresis in response, escalation, and evolving business practice. The authors explain and illustrate why each scenario can occur in practice and describe its positive and negative consequences for long-term profitability. The authors propose to use multivariate persistence measures to identify which of the four strategic scenarios is taking place and illustrate this approach in the pharmaceutical and packaged-food industries. The results substantiate the authors' proposition that the strategic scenario is a major determinant of marketing effectiveness and long-term profitability. This conclusion sets up a substantial agenda for further research.

Jacobson, Robert, and David A. Aaker
Is Market Share All That It's Cracked Up to Be?
Journal of Marketing 49 (4) (Fall 1985), 11–22.
1985 Alpha Kappa Psi Award Winner (as of 1996, the Marketing Science Institute H. Paul Root Award)

The market share-ROI relationship is examined to determine the extent of the causal versus spurious association. By making use of the PIMS database, it is found that a large proportion of the association is spurious in the sense that both market share and ROI are the joint outcome of some third factor(s). The direct impact of market share on ROI is found to be much smaller than previous studies have indicated. It is suggested that too much emphasis is placed on market share and that more attention needs to be focused on other fundamentals.

Mela, Carl F., Sunil Gupta, and Donald R. Lehmann
The Long-Term Impact of Promotion and Advertising on Consumer Brand Choice
Journal of Marketing Research 34 (2) (May 1997), 248–61.
1998 Paul E. Green Award Winner and 2002 William F. O'Dell Award Winner
An earlier version of this paper appeared as MSI Report No. 96–127.

The authors examine the long-term effects of promotion and advertising on consumers' brand choice behavior. They use 8 ¼ years of panel data for a frequently purchased packaged good to address two questions: (1) Do consumers' responses to marketing mix variables, such as price, change over a long period of time? (2) If yes, are these changes associated with changes in manufacturers' advertising and retailers' promotional policies? Using these results, the authors draw implications for manufacturers' pricing, advertising, and promotion policies. The authors use a two-stage approach, which permits them to assess the medium-term (quarterly) effects of advertising and promotion as well as their long-term (i.e., over an infinite horizon) effects. Their results are consistent with the hypotheses that consumers become more price and promotion sensitive over time because of reduced advertising and increased promotions.

Nijs, Vincent R., Marnik G. Dekimpe, Jan-Benedict E. M. Steenkamp, and Dominique M. Hanssens
The Category-Demand Effects of Price Promotions
Marketing Science 20 (1) (Winter 2001), 1–22.
Co-winner of the 2001 John D. C. Little Award and 2002 Frank M. Bass Dissertation Paper Award Winner
An earlier version of this paper appeared as MSI Report No. 00–109, "The Short- and Long-run Category Demand Effects of Price Promotions."

Although price promotions have increased in both commercial use and quantity of academic research over the last decade, most of the attention has been focused on their effects on brand choice and brand sales. By contrast, little is known about the conditions under which price promotions expand short-run and long-run category demand, even though the benefits of category expansion can be substantial to manufacturers and retailers alike. This paper studies the category-demand effects of consumer price promotions across 560 consumer product categories over a 4-year period. The data describe national sales in Dutch supermarkets and cover virtually the entire marketing mix, i.e., prices, promotions, advertising, distribution, and new-product activity. We focus on the estimation of main effects (i.e., the dynamic category expansive impact of price promotions) as well as the moderating effects of marketing intensity and competition (both conduct and structure) on short- and long-run promotional effectiveness.

The research design uses modern multivariate time-series analysis to disentangle short-run and long-run effects. First, we conduct a series of unit-root tests to determine whether or not category demand is stationary or evolving over time. The results are incorporated in the specification of vector-autoregressive models with exogenous variables (VARX models). The impulse-response functions derived from these VARX models provide estimates of the short- and long-term effects of price promotions on category demand. These estimates, in turn, are used as dependent variables in a series of second-stage regressions that assess the explanatory power of marketing intensity and competition. Several model validation tests support the robustness of the empirical findings. We present our results in the form of empirical generalizations on the main effects of price promotions on category demand in the short and the long run and through statistical tests on how these effects change with marketing intensity and competition.

The findings generate an overall picture of the power and limitations of consumer price promotions in expanding category demand, as follows. Category demand is found to be predominantly stationary, either around a fixed mean or a deterministic trend. Although the total net short-term effects of price promotions are generally strong, with an average elasticity of 2.21 and a more conservative median elasticity of 1.75, they rarely exhibit persistent effects. Instead, the effects dissipate over a time period lasting approximately 10 weeks on average, and their long-term impact is essentially zero. By contrast, the successful introduction of new products into a category is more frequently associated with a permanent category-demand increase. Several moderating effects on price-promotion effectiveness exist. More frequent promotions increase their effectiveness, but only in the short run. The use of nonprice advertising reduces the category-demand effects of price promotions, both in the short run and in the long run.

Competitive structure matters as well: The less oligopolistic the category, the smaller the short-run effectiveness of price promotions. At the same time, we find that the dominant form of competitive reaction, either in price promotion or in advertising, is no reaction. Short-run category-demand effectiveness of price promotions is lower in categories experiencing major new-product introductions. Finally, both the short- and long-run price promotion effectiveness is higher in perishable product categories. The paper discusses several managerial implications of these empirical findings and suggests various avenues for future research. Overall, we conclude that the power of price promotions lies primarily in the preservation of the status quo in the category.

Rust, Roland T., Katherine N. Lemon, and Valarie A. Zeithaml

Return on Marketing: Using Customer Equity to Focus Marketing Strategy

Journal of Marketing 68 (1) (January 2004), 109–27.

2004 Marketing Science Institute H. Paul Root Award Winner

The authors present a unified strategic framework that enables competing marketing strategy options to be traded off on the basis of projected financial return, which is operationalized as the change in a firm's customer equity relative to the incremental expenditure necessary to produce the change. The change in the firm's customer equity is the change in its current and future customers' lifetime values, summed across all customers in the industry. Each customer's lifetime value results from the frequency of category purchases, average quantity of purchase, and brand-switching patterns combined with the firm's contribution margin. The brand-switching matrix can be estimated from either longitudinal panel data or cross-sectional survey data, using a logit choice model. Firms can analyze drivers that have the greatest impact, compare the drivers' performance with that of competitors' drivers, and project return on investment from improvements in the drivers. To demonstrate how the approach can be implemented in a specific corporate setting and to show the methods used to test and validate the model, the authors illustrate a detailed application of the approach by using data from the airline industry. Their framework enables what-if evaluation of marketing returns on investment, which can include such criteria as return on quality, return on advertising, return on loyalty programs, and even return on corporate citizenship, given a particular shift in customer perceptions. This enables the firm to focus marketing efforts on strategic initiatives that generate the greatest return.

Rust, Roland T., Christine Moorman, and Peter R. Dickson

Getting Return on Quality: Revenue Expansion, Cost Reduction, or Both?

Journal of Marketing 66 (4) (October 2002), 7–24.

2002 Marketing Science Institute H. Paul Root Award Winner

An earlier version of this paper appeared as MSI Report No. 00–120, "Getting Returns from Service Quality: Is the Conventional Wisdom Wrong?"

Financial benefits from quality may be derived from revenue expansion, cost reduction, or both simultaneously. The literature on both market orientation and customer satisfaction provides considerable support for the effectiveness of the revenue expansion perspective, whereas the literature on both quality and operations provides equally impressive support for the effectiveness of the cost reduction perspective. There is, however, little evidence for the effectiveness of attempting both revenue expansion and cost reduction simultaneously, and some of what little empirical and theoretical literature is available suggests that emphasizing both simultaneously may not work. In a study of managers in firms seeking to obtain a financial return from quality improvements, the authors address the issue of which quality profitability emphasis (revenue expansion, cost reduction, or both) is most effective. The authors examine firm performance using managers' reports of firm performance and longitudinal secondary data on firm profitability and stock returns. Although it is clear that no company can neglect either revenue expansion or cost reduction, the empirical results suggest that firms that adopt primarily a revenue expansion emphasis perform better than firms that try to emphasize cost reduction and better than firms that try to emphasize both revenue expansion and cost reduction simultaneously. The results have implications with respect to how both theory and practice view organizational efforts to achieve financial returns from quality improvements.

Rust, Roland T., Anthony J. Zahorik, and Timothy L. Keiningham
Return on Quality (ROQ): Making Service Quality Financially Accountable

Journal of Marketing 59 (2) (April 1995), 58–70.
1995 Alpha Kappa Psi Award Winner (as of 1996, the Marketing Science Institute H. Paul Root Award)
An earlier version of this paper appeared as MSI Report No. 94–106.

Many companies have been disappointed by a lack of results from their quality efforts. The financial benefits of quality, which had been assumed as a matter of faith in the "religion of quality," are now being seriously questioned by cost-cutting executives, who cite the highly publicized financial failures of some companies prominent in the quality movement. In this increasingly results-oriented environment, managers must now justify their quality improvement efforts financially. The authors present the "return on quality" approach, which is based on the assumptions that (1) quality is an investment, (2) quality efforts must be financially accountable, (3) it is possible to spend too much on quality, and (4) not all quality expenditures are equally valid. The authors then provide a managerial framework that can be used to guide quality improvement efforts. This framework has several attractive features, including ensured managerial relevance and financial accountability.

Srivastava, Rajendra K., Tasadduq A. Shervani, and Liam Fahey

Market-Based Assets and Shareholder Value: A Framework for Analysis

Journal of Marketing 62 (1) (January 1998), 2–18.

1998 Harold H. Maynard Award Winner and 1998 Marketing Science Institute H. Paul Root Award Winner

The authors develop a conceptual framework of the marketing-finance interface and discuss its implications for the theory and practice of marketing. The framework proposes that marketing is concerned with the task of developing and managing market-based assets, or assets that arise from the commingling of the firm with entities in its external environment. Examples of market-based assets include customer relationships, channel relationships, and partner relationships. Market-based assets, in turn, increase shareholder value by accelerating and enhancing cash flows, lowering the volatility and vulnerability of cash flows, and increasing the residual value of cash flows.

Webster, Frederick E., Jr., James A. Largay III, and Clyde P. Stickney

The Impact of Inflation Accounting on Marketing Decisions

Journal of Marketing 44 (4) (Fall 1980), 9–17.

1980 Alpha Kappa Psi Award Winner (as of 1996, the Marketing Science Institute H. Paul Root Award)

Persistent inflation in the American economy has led accounting rule makers to require large firms to report the effects of inflation on certain of their financial statement data. At present, these adjusted data are to be presented as supplementary disclosures under Statement of Financial Accounting Standards No. 33, "Financial Reporting and Changing Prices." One major result will be significant changes in cost estimates and asset valuations. The changes in financial accounting requirements are likely to be reflected almost immediately in managerial accounting procedures, with specific implications for marketing decisions in such areas as new product introduction, pricing strategy, and the valuation of individual customers and market segments. The authors describe the new accounting data briefly and, using examples, illustrate the implications for marketing managers.

Additional Relevant Papers: Metrics Linking Marketing to Financial Performance

Ailawadi, Kusum L., Donald R. Lehmann, and Scott A. Neslin
Revenue Premium as an Outcome Measure of Brand Equity
Journal of Marketing 67 (4) (October 2003), 1–17. See page 28 for abstract.
2003 Harold H. Maynard Award Winner

Hunt, Shelby D., and Robert M. Morgan
The Comparative Advantage Theory of Competition
Journal of Marketing 59 (2) (April 1995), 1–15. See page 179 for abstract.
1995 Harold H. Maynard Award Winner

Reinartz, Werner J., and V. Kumar
The Impact of Customer Relationship Characteristics on Profitable Lifetime Duration
Journal of Marketing 67 (1) (January 2003), 77–99. See page 58 for abstract.
2003 Marketing Science Institute H. Paul Root Award Winner

Schmittlein, David C., and Robert A. Peterson
Customer Base Analysis: An Industrial Purchase Process Application
Marketing Science 13 (1) (Winter 1994), 41–67. See page 58 for abstract.
1994 John D. C. Little Award Winner

Sultan, Fareena, John U. Farley, and Donald R. Lehmann
A Meta-Analysis of Applications of Diffusion Models
Journal of Marketing Research 27 (1) (February 1990), 70–7. See page 20 for abstract.
1995 William F. O'Dell Award Winner

4

Managing Relationships with Customers and Organizations

This chapter covers prize-winning papers on customer relationship management (CRM), with a special emphasis on managing interorganizational relationships (that is, business-to-business relationships or relationships within a channel, supply chain, or network). The papers tackle two major research challenges. First, marketers have displayed an enduring interest in how organizations can develop relationships with customers over time and how these relationships can be effectively managed. Consequently, one group of prize-winning papers has studied customer acquisition, customer retention, and revenue expansion, as well as the optimal allocation of resources to the underlying activities that create, build, and sustain relationships over time. Second, marketers have been especially interested in interorganizational relationships because—until the advent of electronic commerce, with its potential for precise (one-to-one) targeting of marketing activities—business-to-business relationships have been the most fruitful context for the application of the principles of CRM. Consequently, a second group of prize-winning papers has studied the implementation of CRM principles in business-to-business relationships. These papers have tended to have a strategic orientation and have reflected the notion that a coherent set of cross-functional activities is required to create, build, and sustain relationships.

Principles of Customer Relationship Management

Customer Acquisition, Retention, and Revenue Expansion
Research on CRM is a natural evolution of marketers' long-standing interest in understanding how relationships with individual customers are created, built, and sustained over time. This research stream began with investigations into how customers formed their assessments of products (goods and services). The service

quality literature developed around the notion that perceived quality is powerfully influenced by the difference between expectations and experience. Boulding et al. (1993) brought together two streams of service quality research when they showed that both expectations as predictions (expectations about what will happen) and normative expectations (expectations about what should happen, often based on communications from the service provider) are important in determining perceived service quality.

Spreng, MacKenzie, and Olshavsky (1996) extended that line of inquiry with a model of satisfaction that included two standards—predictive expectations and desires—and showed that congruence with desires is a key antecedent of satisfaction. Their study also showed the complex effects of expectations. Fournier and Mick's (1999) study of the lived experience of customer satisfaction showed that comparisons between expectations and actual experience were insufficient to explain customer satisfaction. The authors proposed a new satisfaction paradigm that acknowledged the lack or instability of comparison standards, the presence of simultaneous and sequential satisfaction models over time, and the sociocultural and emotional character of an individual's satisfaction response.

Complementing the development of behavioral process models, marketers have built models that predict (rather than explain) customer behavior over time. In an industrial purchase context, Schmittlein and Peterson (1994) used past purchase behavior—that is, data on the frequency, timing, and dollar value of past purchases—to predict likely future purchase patterns. They were able to show that their "customer base analysis" effectively predicted purchase patterns for different key customer groups.

Can these models be used to explain and predict individual customer profitability? Initially, researchers tackled this question by estimating individual customers' lifetime values. (Customer lifetime value can refer to revenue or cash flow stream, as well as contribution margin or profit stream.) This task is doable, but it can be challenging to move from the calculation of individual customers' lifetime revenues to individual customers' profitability. Niraj, Gupta, and Narasimhan (2001) demonstrated how to move from current profitability to lifetime value for an intermediary in a supply chain, given that costs in a supply chain are cumulative and that customers at different points in the chain have heterogeneous purchasing characteristics.

Linkages to (Short-Run) Profitability

Marketers are especially interested in identifying which variables are the best predictors of customer lifetime profitability. Reinartz and Kumar (2003) compared traditional models that consider frequency, timing, and monetary value of purchases with models that show how managerial decision variables influence the profitability of customers over time; they concluded that the latter were superior.

Direct marketing to consumers is a useful context in which to study how managerial decisions influence customer behavior and profitability because there is a well-defined set of tactical marketing variables that are under managerial control. Several prize-winning papers show that when direct marketing vehicles such as catalogs, interactive home shopping, and direct mail tailor their messages to individual consumers, they can generate revenues and profits that are superior to those generated by traditional marketing methods (Ansari and Mela 2003; Bult and Wansbeek 1995).

Customer Relationship Management and Shareholder Value

As research on CRM has matured, marketers' attention has shifted from a consideration of how it influences short-run profitability to a consideration of how it influences long-run profitability and shareholder value. Recent research has conceptualized the customer relationship as a market-based asset, thereby linking research on CRM with marketing metrics and influencing subsequent work. This shift in emphasis has implied a movement toward more strategic, unified models and away from models that focus on tactical decision variables. These papers, which straddle the marketing-finance interface, often use return on investment to evaluate strategic investments. Recent research has examined the links between strategic investments (e.g., in quality, advertising, loyalty programs, corporate citizenship) and "customer equity" or shareholder value—that is, the sum of current and future customer lifetime values. That research stream is described in Chapter 3, "Metrics Linking Marketing to Financial Performance."

Implementation of Customer Relationship Management in Supply Chains or Networks

An early paper by Stern and Reve (1980) offered a conceptual framework for studying supply chains or networks. They emphasized that an analysis of both economic and sociopolitical determinants of channel member behavior is necessary to evaluate alternative approaches to managing business-to-business relationships.

Managing Business-to-Business Relationships

Efficient and effective supply chains have become increasingly important for business success. Over the past 20 years, transaction cost analysis (TCA) has become an important conceptual tool for studying questions concerning interorganizational relationships. Rindfleisch and Heide (1997) provided an excellent synthesis and integration of TCA research. Two important constructs in understanding interorganizational relationships are trust and commitment. Anderson and Weitz (1992) considered how commitment depends on self-reported and perceived "pledges" (i.e., idiosyncratic investments and contractual terms), communication, and relationship characteristics. Their research is particularly noteworthy because they studied 378 manufacturer–industrial distributor pairs and were able to model the antecedents and consequences of each party's perception of the other party's commitment.

Governance Strategies

Governance strategies, such as integration or control strategies, are used to structure and regulate the conduct of interorganizational relationships. Research on this topic draws on theoretical work in organization theory, law, and economics. Heide (1994) reviewed and synthesized these perspectives and developed a typology that describes the antecedents and consequences of different forms of governance.

Governance strategies can constrain the latitude of decisions by channel members (e.g., via formal contracts) or they can attempt to achieve voluntary compliance (e.g., via communication). Lusch and Brown (1996) showed that wholesaler-distributors and suppliers develop different types of contracts to coordinate their activities, depending on whether the wholesaler is dependent on the supplier, the supplier is dependent on the wholesaler, or there is high bilateral dependency. Mohr, Fisher, and Nevin's (1996) research indicated that when levels of integration or manufacturer control are high, the effect of collaborative communication on performance outcomes (e.g., satisfaction, commitment) is weaker than when integration or control is low. Under conditions of low integration or low control, dealers appear to be more receptive to and influenced by collaborative communication—suggesting the possibility that collaborative communication may serve as a governance structure in its own right.

Synthesis

Research on customer management strategies and tactics has broadened and deepened in recent years. The emerging view is that customer management requires cross-functional integration of all activities within the organization and across the network of firms that collaborate to generate customer value if it is to create shareholder value for the firms. Much more work must be done to understand the circumstances under which customer management strategies and tactics will be effective. For example, with the advent of e-commerce, research has shifted to a consideration of multichannel environments. Recently, Alba et al. (1997) described the potential consumer benefits and limitations of an Internet channel as compared with traditional store and catalog retail channels and discussed the types of firms that are well positioned to provide these benefits.

Research Priorities

Consistent with recent research trends, MSI's 2004–2006 research priorities highlight key strategic issues (as opposed to tactical issues) associated with managing customers, with an emphasis on the implementation and assessment of CRM activities. The new priorities reflect the notion that customer management is a natural evolution from well-established market segmentation and target-marketing activities, but there is a focus on how customer relationships are managed over time and across touch points. The same research priorities arise in business-to-business and business-to-customer contexts, although there are naturally differences in how they might be investigated.

The 2004–2006 priorities include:

- measuring and predicting the lifetime value of customers
- segmenting and managing by the type of relationship desired by the customer (consumer or firm)
- managing and maintaining customers through multiple channels

Customer portfolio management is a relatively new research priority. Customer portfolio management goes beyond a consideration of the tradeoffs involved in balancing investments in acquisition and retention and raises the broader question of how an organization creates and manages a portfolio of relationships with customers that matches its products portfolio—thereby enhancing shareholder value.

Abstracts: Managing Relationships with Customers and Organizations

Alba, Joseph, John Lynch, Barton Weitz, Chris Janiszewski, Richard Lutz, Alan Sawyer, and Stacy Wood

Interactive Home Shopping: Consumer, Retailer, and Manufacturer Incentives to Participate in Electronic Marketplaces

Journal of Marketing 61 (3) (July 1997), 38–53.

1997 Marketing Science Institute H. Paul Root Award Winner and 2005 Louis W. Stern Award Winner

An earlier version of this paper appeared as MSI Report No. 97–105, "Interactive Home Shopping and the Retail Industry."

The authors examine the implications of electronic shopping for consumers, retailers, and manufacturers. They assume that near-term technological developments will offer consumers unparalleled opportunities to locate and compare product offerings. They examine these advantages as a function of typical consumer goals and the types of products and services being sought and offer conclusions regarding consumer incentives and disincentives to purchase through interactive home shopping vis-à-vis traditional retail formats. The authors discuss implications for industry structure as they pertain to competition among retailers, competition among manufacturers, and retailer-manufacturer relationships.

Anderson, Erin, and Barton Weitz

The Use of Pledges to Build and Sustain Commitment in Distribution Channels

Journal of Marketing Research 29 (1) (February 1992), 18–34.

2000 Louis W. Stern Award Winner

An earlier version of this paper appeared as MSI Report No. 91–114.

Commitment in channel relationships is modeled as a function of (1) each party's perception of the other party's commitment, (2) self-reported and perceived pledges (idiosyncratic investments and contractual terms) made by each party, and (3) other factors such as communication level, reputation, and relationship history. A dyadic model represented by a simultaneous equation system is estimated with data from 378 pairs of manufacturers and industrial distributors. The results indicate that one type of pledge, idiosyncratic investments, has a strong effect on the commitment of both parties to the relationship. In addition, each party's commitment is affected by the perceived commitment of the other party. Finally, idiosyncratic investments signal commitment, affecting each party's perceptions of the other party's commitment.

Ansari, Asim, and Carl F. Mela
E-Customization
Journal of Marketing Research 40 (2) (May 2003), 131–45.
Co-winner of the 2004 Paul E. Green Award

Customized communications have the potential to reduce information overload and aid customer decisions, and the highly relevant products that result from customization can form the cornerstone of enduring customer relationships. In spite of such potential benefits, few models exist in the marketing literature to exploit the Internet's unique ability to design communications or marketing programs at the individual level. The authors develop a statistical and optimization approach for customization of information on the Internet. The authors use clickstream data from users at one of the top ten most trafficked Web sites to estimate the model and optimize the design and content of such communications for each user. The authors apply the model to the context of permission-based e-mail marketing, in which the objective is to customize the design and content of the e-mail to increase Web site traffic. The analysis suggests that the content-targeting approach can potentially increase the expected number of click-throughs by 62%.

Boulding, William, Ajay Kalra, Richard Staelin, and Valarie A. Zeithaml
A Dynamic Process Model of Service Quality: From Expectations to Behavioral Intentions
Journal of Marketing Research 30 (1) (February 1993), 7–27.
Co-winner of the 1998 William F. O'Dell Award
An earlier version of this paper appeared as MSI Report No. 92–121, "Conceptualizing and Testing a Dynamic Process Model of Service Quality"

Relying on a Bayesian-like framework, the authors develop a behavioral process model of perceived service quality. Perceptions of the dimensions of service quality are viewed to be a function of a customer's prior expectations of what will and what should transpire during a service encounter, as well as the customer's most recent contact with the service delivery system. These perceptions of quality dimensions form the basis for a person's overall quality perception, which in turn predicts the person's intended behaviors. The authors first test this model with data from a longitudinal laboratory experiment. Then they develop a method for estimating the model with one-time survey data, and reestimate the model using such data collected in a field study. Empirical findings from the two tests of the model indicate, among other things, that the two different types of expectations have opposing effects on perceptions of service quality and that service quality perceptions positively affect intended behaviors.

Bult, Jan Roelf, and Tom Wansbeek
Optimal Selection for Direct Mail
Marketing Science 14 (4) (Autumn 1995), 378–94.
1995 Frank M. Bass Dissertation Paper Award Winner

Direct marketing (mail) is a growing area of marketing practice, yet the academic journals contain very little research on this topic. The most important issue for direct marketers is how to sample targets from a population for a direct mail campaign. Although some selection methods are described in the literature, there seems to be not a single paper discussing the analytical and statistical aspects involved. The objective of this paper is to introduce a comprehensive methodology for the selection of targets from a mailing list for direct mail. At least theoretically, this methodology leads to more efficient selection procedures than the existing ones. The latter are not based on an optimal selection strategy, whereas we explicitly take the profit function into account. By equating marginal costs and marginal returns we determine which households should receive a mailing in order to maximize expected profit. In the empirical part we show that our methodology has great predictive accuracy and generates higher net returns than traditional approaches.

Fournier, Susan, and David Glen Mick
Rediscovering Satisfaction
Journal of Marketing 63 (4) (October 1999), 5–23.
1999 Harold H. Maynard Award Winner
An earlier version of this paper appeared as MSI Report No. 95–104, "Technological Consumer Products in Everyday Life: Ownership, Meaning, and Satisfaction."

The authors present a phenomenological and longitudinal investigation of satisfaction, as revealed through consumers' ownership experiences with technological products. The study seeks to serve a provocative role in this mature research area by stepping back from the historically dominant comparison standards paradigm to question, invigorate, and, in certain ways, redirect satisfaction research along emergent lines. Although results show that the dominant paradigm of satisfaction and its competing models (i. e., those based on the confirmation/disconfirmation of preconsumption standards) are distinctly operative in some of the consumer cases, they are also found to be insufficient or even irrelevant in others. The authors consider several theoretical extensions in light of this learning and induct a new satisfaction paradigm. Overall, the findings support a more holistic, context-dependent, and dynamic process of satisfaction. This process is revealed as a multi-model, multi-modal blend of motivations, cognitions, emotions, and meanings, embedded in sociocultural settings, which transforms during progressive and regressive consumer-product interactions.

Heide, Jan B.
Interorganizational Governance in Marketing Channels
Journal of Marketing 58 (1) (January 1994), 71–85.
2001 Louis W. Stern Award Winner

Relationship management rapidly is becoming a central research paradigm in the marketing channels literature. A growing body of conceptual and empirical literature addresses different aspects of interfirm relationships, building in part on recent theoretical developments in organization theory, law, and economics. Interestingly, however, some of these theoretical frameworks make radically different assumptions about the nature of interfirm relationships, though these differences to date have not been examined systematically in the marketing literature. The author reviews these theoretical perspectives and develops a formal typology of approaches to relationship management. Specifically, he develops a typology of three different forms of governance, which vary systematically in terms of how specific interfirm processes are carried out. He also discusses the antecedents of different relationship forms and shows the results of a preliminary empirical test.

Lusch, Robert F., and James R. Brown
Interdependency, Contracting, and Relational Behavior in Marketing Channels
Journal of Marketing 60 (4) (October 1996), 19–38.
Co-winner of the 1996 Harold H. Maynard Award and 2002 Louis W. Stern Award Winner

The dependency structure between wholesale-distributors and their major suppliers is posited to influence the type of contract—explicit and normative—used. In turn, dependency structure and type of contract is hypothesized to influence wholesale-distributor performance. This process occurs both directly and indirectly through some intermediate constructs, such as long-term orientation, relationship length, and relational behavior. The authors investigate three dependency structures: wholesaler dependent on supplier, supplier dependent on wholesaler, and high bilateral dependency. They obtain empirical support for many of the hypothesized linkages.

Mohr, Jakki J., Robert J. Fisher, and John R. Nevin

Collaborative Communication in Interfirm Relationships: Moderating Effects of Integration and Control

Journal of Marketing 60 (3) (July 1996), 103–15.
2003 Louis W. Stern Award Winner
An earlier version of this paper appeared as MSI Report No. 94–119, "The Role of Communication Strategy in Channel Member Performance: Is More Collaborative Communication Better?"

Governance strategies, such as integration or control, structure and regulate the conduct of parties in exchange relationships; as such, they serve to constrain the latitude of the decision making of channel partners. Similarly, collaborative communication can be used to create an atmosphere of mutual support, thereby creating volitional compliance between partners. The authors develop a model that addresses the interrelationships of governance and communication and examine the effects of collaborative communication on channel outcomes (the dealer's perceptions of commitment to, satisfaction with, and coordination of activities with a focal manufacturer) across various levels of integration and control. Based on survey data collected from a national sample of computer dealers, the findings indicate that when levels of integration or manufacturer control are high, the effect of collaborative communication on outcomes is weaker than when integration or control is low.

Niraj, Rakesh, Mahendra Gupta, and Chakravarthi Narasimhan

Customer Profitability in a Supply Chain

Journal of Marketing 65 (3) (July 2001), 1–16.
2001 Marketing Science Institute H. Paul Root Award Winner
An earlier version of this paper appeared as MSI Report No. 99–125.

Estimating current profitability at the individual customer level is important to distinguish the more profitable customers from the less profitable ones. This is also a first step in developing estimates of customers' lifetime values. This exercise, however, takes on additional complexities when applied to an intermediary in a supply chain, such as a distributor, because the costs of servicing a retail customer include not only those incurred directly in servicing this customer but also those incurred by the distributor in dealing with its own vendors for goods supplied to this customer. The authors develop a general model and measurement methodology to relate customer profitability to customer characteristics in a supply chain. The authors show how heterogeneity in customer purchasing characteristics leads to important profit implications and illustrate the implementation of the methodology using data from a large distributor that supplies to grocery and other retail businesses.

Reinartz, Werner J., and V. Kumar

The Impact of Customer Relationship Characteristics on Profitable Lifetime Duration

Journal of Marketing 67 (1) (January 2003), 77–99.

2003 Marketing Science Institute H. Paul Root Award Winner

The authors develop a framework that incorporates projected profitability of customers in the computation of lifetime duration. Furthermore, the authors identify factors under a manager's control that explain the variation in the profitable lifetime duration. They also compare other frameworks with the traditional methods such as the recency, frequency, and monetary value framework and past customer value and illustrate the superiority of the proposed framework. Finally, the authors develop several key implications that can be of value to decision makers in managing customer relationships.

Rindfleisch, Aric, and Jan B. Heide

Transaction Cost Analysis: Past, Present, and Future Applications

Journal of Marketing 61 (4) (October 1997), 30–54.

1997 Harold H. Maynard Award Winner and 2004 Louis W. Stern Award Winner

Over the past decade, transaction cost analysis (TCA) has received considerable attention in the marketing literature. Marketing scholars have made important contributions in extending and refining TCA's original conceptual framework. The authors provide a synthesis and integration of recent contributions to TCA by both marketers and scholars in related disciplines, an evaluation of recent critiques of TCA, and an agenda for further research on TCA.

Schmittlein, David C., and Robert A. Peterson

Customer Base Analysis: An Industrial Purchase Process Application

Marketing Science 13 (1) (Winter 1994), 41–67.

1994 John D. C. Little Award Winner

Customer base analysis is concerned with using the observed past purchase behavior of customers to understand their current and likely future purchase patterns. More specifically, as developed in Schmittlein et al. (1987), customer base analysis uses data on the frequency, timing, and dollar value of each customer's past purchases to infer (1) the number of customers currently active, (2) how that number has changed over time, (3) which individual customers are most likely still active, (4) how much longer each is likely to remain an active customer, and (5) how many purchases can be expected from each during any future time period of interest. In this paper we empirically validate the model proposed by Schmittlein et al. In doing so, we provide one of the few applications of stochastic models to industrial purchase processes and industrial marketing decisions. Besides showing that the model does capture key aspects of the purchase process, we also present a more effective parameter estimation method and some results regarding sampling properties of the parameter estimates. Finally, we extend the model to explicitly incorporate dollar volume of past purchases. Our results indicate that this kind of customer base analysis can be both effective in predicting purchase patterns and in generating insights into how key customer groups differ. The link of both these benefits to industrial marketing decision making is also discussed.

Spreng, Richard A., Scott B. MacKenzie, and Richard W. Olshavsky
A Reexamination of the Determinants of Consumer Satisfaction
Journal of Marketing 60 (3) (July 1996), 15–32.
Co-winner of the 1996 Harold H. Maynard Award

Although the "disconfirmation of expectations" model continues to dominate research and managerial practice, several limitations indicate that it is not a complete picture of satisfaction formation. The authors propose a new model of the satisfaction formation process that builds on the disconfirmation paradigm by specifying a more comprehensive model that includes two standards in a single model and specifically incorporates the impact of marketing communication. An empirical test of the model provides support for the hypothesized relationships and a better understanding of the mechanisms that produce satisfaction.

Stern, Louis W., and Torger Reve
Distribution Channels as Political Economies: A Framework for Comparative Analysis
Journal of Marketing 44 (3) (Summer 1980), 52–64.
Co-winner of the 1980 Harold H. Maynard Award

This paper presents a unifying framework for the analysis of distribution channels which encompasses both economic and sociopolitical determinants of channel member behavior and provides a suitable departure point for comparative work. The framework integrates present approaches to the study of marketing channels and provides an essential, but heretofore missing, basis for comprehensive empirical research in the area.

Additional Relevant Papers: Managing Relationships with Customers and Organizations

Balasubramanian, Sridhar

Mail versus Mall: A Strategic Analysis of Competition between Direct Marketers and Conventional Retailers

Marketing Science 17 (3) (Summer 1998), 181–95. See page 172 for abstract.

1998 John D. C. Little Award Winner

Bucklin, Louis P., and Sanjit Sengupta

Organizing Successful Co-Marketing Alliances

Journal of Marketing 57 (2) (April 1993), 32–46. See page 174 for abstract.

1993 Alpha Kappa Psi Award Winner (as of 1996, the Marketing Science Institute H. Paul Root Award)

Choffray, Jean-Marie, and Gary L. Lilien

Assessing Response to Industrial Marketing Strategy

Journal of Marketing 42 (2) (April 1978), 20–31. See page 89 for abstract.

1978 Alpha Kappa Psi Award Winner (as of 1996, the Marketing Science Institute H. Paul Root Award)

Glazer, Rashi

Marketing in an Information-Intensive Environment: Strategic Implications of Knowledge as an Asset

Journal of Marketing 55 (4) (October 1991), 1–19. See page 177 for abstract.

1991 Harold H. Maynard Award Winner

Hunt, Shelby D., and Robert M. Morgan

The Comparative Advantage Theory of Competition

Journal of Marketing 59 (2) (April 1995), 1–15. See page 179 for abstract.

1995 Harold H. Maynard Award Winner

Jacobson, Robert, and David A. Aaker

Is Market Share All That It's Cracked Up to Be?

Journal of Marketing 49 (4) (Fall 1985), 11–22. See page 40 for abstract.

1985 Alpha Kappa Psi Award Winner (as of 1996, the Marketing Science Institute H. Paul Root Award)

Jain, Dipak C., and Naufel J. Vilcassim

Investigating Household Purchase Timing Decisions: A Conditional Hazard Function Approach

Marketing Science 10 (1) (Winter 1991), 1–23. See page 96 for abstract.

1991 John D. C. Little Award Winner

Purohit, Devavrat

Dual Distribution Channels: The Competition between Rental Agencies and Dealers

Marketing Science 16 (3) (Summer 1997), 228–45. See page 182 for abstract.

Co-winner of the 1997 John D. C. Little Award

Rust, Roland T., Katherine N. Lemon, and Valarie A. Zeithaml

Return on Marketing: Using Customer Equity to Focus Marketing Strategy

Journal of Marketing 68 (1) (January 2004), 109–27. See page 43 for abstract.

2004 Marketing Science Institute H. Paul Root Award Winner

Rust, Roland T., Christine Moorman, and Peter R. Dickson

Getting Return on Quality: Revenue Expansion, Cost Reduction, or Both?

Journal of Marketing 66 (4) (October 2002), 7–24. See page 43 for abstract.

2002 Marketing Science Institute H. Paul Root Award Winner

Srivastava, Rajendra K., Tasadduq A. Shervani, and Liam Fahey

Market-Based Assets and Shareholder Value: A Framework for Analysis

Journal of Marketing 62 (1) (January 1998), 2–18. See page 45 for abstract.

1998 Harold H. Maynard Award Winner and 1998 Marketing Science Institute H. Paul Root Award Winner

Vargo, Stephen L., and Robert F. Lusch

Evolving to a New Dominant Logic for Marketing

Journal of Marketing 68 (1) (January 2004), 1–17. See page 77 for abstract.

2004 Harold H. Maynard Award Winner

5

The Role of Marketing

The role of marketing has changed over time, reflecting fundamental shifts in how people think about what marketing can and should be, its appropriate subject matter, its role in society, and how it should be approached and advanced. For example, MSI is currently interested in commissioning studies on specific questions concerning the role of marketing within companies, such as how to organize marketing, implement reward systems, manage marketing as a value creator rather than an expense, and improve utilization of marketing information. In past years, by contrast, research took a broader perspective, considering marketing as a system and dealing with topics such as the role of marketing in society. In this chapter, we group the award-winning papers into five major categories or topics that (roughly) correspond to the chronological order in which the topics first arose and were debated in the marketing community. They are: marketing and society, the concept of marketing and its definition, toward a general theory of marketing, criteria for the generation and testing of marketing theories, and the role of marketing within the company.

Marketing and Society

Almost forty years ago, marketers began to take an intense interest in issues relevant to marketing and society. The first of four reports that were developed by the American Marketing Association (AMA) Task Force on Research on Basic Problems in Marketing was an award-winning paper titled "Impact of Government upon the Market System." In this paper, Grether and Holloway (1967) proposed examining how government affects both the marketing system as a whole and specific marketing subsystems. Subsequently, researchers addressed questions such as whether the poor pay more (Goodman 1968), what the marketing implications of the internationalization of American business are (Leighton 1970), how marketing can be used to promote social objectives (Kotler and Zaltman 1971), and how marketers can be involved in market actions that balance the national economic policy of competition with ecological, social, environmental, and holistic concerns (Grether 1974). The notion of macromarketing also emerged during this decade (Bartels and Jenkins 1977).

The Concept of Marketing and Its Definition

From the late 1960s on, marketers were also wrestling with whether marketing was a pervasive social activity, an organizational activity, or both. Kotler and Levy (1969) argued that marketing principles were relevant to all entities having customer groups, including nonprofit organizations, persons, and ideas. Subsequently, Kotler (1972) argued that marketing was the disciplined task of creating and offering values to others, and thus could be broadened to include transactions between an organization and all of its "publics" (i.e., stakeholders). He also determined that the fundamental concept underlying marketing was exchange. This research stream led to a consideration of whether the definition of marketing should be changed (Tucker 1974).

Toward a General Theory of Marketing

Hunt (1976) suggested that a new model of the scope of marketing, later called the "three dichotomies" model of marketing, might help resolve questions about the nature of marketing and marketing science. Leone and Schultz (1980) argued that scientific generalizations had to precede creation of a general theory of marketing. Subsequently, Hunt (1983) considered the nature of theory in marketing and discussed what a general theory of marketing would explain and predict.

Criteria for the Generation and Testing of Marketing Theories

Reflecting significant changes under way in marketing, several award-winning papers attempted to develop criteria for rigorously developing, testing, and evaluating theories in marketing. Bagozzi (1984) tackled how marketing theories should be constructed and contrasted positivist and realist approaches. Arndt (1985) argued that marketing thinking was dominated by the logical empiricist paradigm and suggested that marketers should consider alternative paradigms that would better capture subjective experiences, conflicts, and liberating forces. Their ideas are reflected and expanded in the award-winning papers described Chapter 6, "Research Tools."

The Role of Marketing within the Company

Organizational Climate and Rewards

Although managers sometimes view marketing and sales as existing in functional silos, this viewpoint is not shared by academics. Among the marketing scholars who have dealt with sales are Churchill, Ford, and Walker (1976), who studied the relationship between organizational climate and job satisfaction, leading to recommendations for improving salesforce morale. Naturally, compensation has been of particular interest, especially the question of what type of compensation plan (straight salary, straight commission, or combination) is appropriate in what situation. Basu et al. (1985) concluded that a salesperson's salary (as a percentage of total compensation) should increase as uncertainty, the marginal cost of production, and the attractiveness of alternative job opportunities increase.

Marketing and Corporate Strategy

Several award-winning papers have examined how marketing relates to business strategy and strategy planning and implementation. Anderson (1982) proposed a theory of the firm that specified how marketing and the other functional areas should contribute to goal setting and the strategic planning process. Walker and Ruekert (1987) considered how different marketing structures, processes, and policies influence the overall performance of different business strategies. Webster (1992) argued that the emergence of new organization forms, such as strategic partnerships and networks, required a new conception of marketing, one focused on managing strategic partnerships in the value chain and delivering value to customers. He viewed customer relationships as a company's key strategic resource.

In an early paper that focused on strategy at the functional level, Buell (1975) described a shift in the locus of decision making in consumer goods companies: product managers gained planning and coordination authority while their authority to make decisions (e.g., about advertising) was restricted. Many years later, Varadarajan, Jayachandran, and White (2001) examined how marketing strategy changes when a firm transforms itself, through divestiture, from a business portfolio of unrelated businesses to one composed of fewer and related businesses.

They found that such firms became more customer and competitor oriented, had greater seller concentration, were more innovative, and placed greater emphasis on advertising than on sales promotion, while their cultures were often more externally oriented. Interestingly, they also found that the locus of decision making for marketing strategy may shift up, to senior management levels.

Market Orientation

Kohli and Jaworski (1990) investigated how companies should implement the marketing concept. After extensive field interviews with managers, they proposed a new construct, market orientation, and discussed its antecedents and consequences. Three years later, they followed up with a second paper (Jaworski and Kohli 1993). Based on their examination of data from two national samples, they concluded that there was a relation between market orientation and overall business performance, and that this relation held under differing conditions of market turbulence, technological turbulence, and intensity of competition. They also related market orientation to employees' organizational commitment. Among the factors they identified that accounted for differences in companies' market orientation were top managers' emphasis on the orientation, top managers' risk aversion, and the presence or absence of interdepartmental conflict, connectedness, centralization, and a reward system orientation.

Day (1994) addressed how market orientation could be achieved and maintained. He argued that the most distinctive features of market-driven organizations are their market-sensing and customer-linking capabilities, and he offered a comprehensive program for enhancing those capabilities. Menon et al. (1999) examined the marketing strategy-making (MSM) process and its effect on firm performance by studying more than 200 decisions relating to the marketing mix. They found that the various components of the MSM process influence strategy creativity, organizational learning, and market performance. They also found that an innovative culture is a fundamental antecedent of an effective MSM process.

Research Priorities

Many of the topics described above are represented in current writings, suggesting that marketers have not arrived at definitive answers to the questions posed in these papers. Most recently, Vargo and Lusch (2004) reviewed many of these issues and argued that a new and fundamentally different logic of marketing is becoming dominant, one that places service—the application of knowledge and skills for the benefit of another party—rather than units of output (goods) at the heart of the exchange process. At the same time, the AMA announced a new definition of marketing that shifted the focus of marketing activities from products to value and relationships.

Looking back over the history of MSI, it is evident that interest in the role of marketing within the company and broader issues, such as marketing and society, ebb and flow over time. The role of marketing in organizations is among MSI's first-tier research priorities for 2004–2006. MSI encourages research on:

- evaluating and controlling marketing performance: the impact of reward systems
- managing marketing as a "value-creator" versus an expense
- growth by expanding business scope
- improving utilization of marketing information by managers
- communicating with and influencing decision makers
- marketing competencies: what makes a great marketer?
- how to organize marketing

Currently, marketing and society is not a first-tier research priority for MSI, but there is a category of third-tier priorities entitled "The Inter-relationship between Marketing and Society." This category includes questions about societal issues (e.g., whether marketing techniques are effective in addressing social problems; what value marketing has for customers and society) and also covers organizational issues (e.g., green marketing, privacy issues, mistrust of marketing, and corporate social responsibility).

The remaining three themes—the concept of marketing and its definition, a general theory of marketing, and criteria for the generation and testing of marketing theories—are not among MSI's research priorities for 2004–2006. This is not entirely surprising as those themes focus on theoretical issues that are of more interest to academics than they are to practitioners.

Abstracts: The Role of Marketing

Anderson, Paul F.

Marketing, Strategic Planning, and the Theory of the Firm

Journal of Marketing 46 (2) (Spring 1982), 15–26.

1982 Harold H. Maynard Award Winner and 1982 Alpha Kappa Psi Award Winner (as of 1996, the Marketing Science Institute H. Paul Root Award)

The strategic planning process is inextricably linked with the issue of corporate goal formulation. It is argued that greater progress will be made in understanding marketing's participation in strategic planning if marketing's role in the goal formulation process can be explicated. Unfortunately, the extant theories of the firm are inadequate in varying degrees for this purpose. A new theory of the firm is proposed that attempts to specify the role of marketing and the other functional areas in the goal setting and strategic planning process.

Arndt, Johan

On Making Marketing Science More Scientific: Role of Orientations, Paradigms, Metaphors, and Puzzle Solving

Journal of Marketing 49 (3) (Summer 1985), 11–23.

1985 Harold H. Maynard Award Winner

Marketing thinking is profoundly dominated by the empiricist world view and the logical empiricist paradigm. This article argues that marketing can be enriched by opening up to alternative paradigms that capture subjective experiences, conflicts, and liberating forces.

Bagozzi, Richard P.

A Prospectus for Theory Construction in Marketing

Journal of Marketing 48 (1) (Winter 1984), 11–29.

1984 Harold H. Maynard Award Winner

This article addresses the question, "How should theories be constructed?" In doing so, two approaches are considered: the classic positivist paradigm and an emerging realist perspective. An attempt is made to develop criteria for representing theories so that they can be more rigorously developed, tested, and evaluated.

Bartels, Robert, and Roger L. Jenkins

Macromarketing

Journal of Marketing 41 (4) (October 1977), 17–20.

1977 Harold H. Maynard Award Winner

A semantic and conceptual challenge: Just what does "Macromarketing" mean—and how can it be used, both in theory and in management?

Basu, Amiya K., Rajiv Lal, V. Srinivasan, and Richard Staelin

Salesforce Compensation Plans: An Agency Theoretic Perspective

Marketing Science 4 (4) (Autumn 1985), 267–91.

1985 Best Paper Award Winner (as of 1988, the John D.C. Little Award)

A theory of salesforce compensation plans is presented where the sales of a product depend not only on the salesperson's effort but also on the uncertainty in the selling environment. The firm chooses a compensation plan to maximize its profit, taking into account the salesperson's likely effort levels under alternative compensation plans and his or her alternative job opportunities. The salesperson (agent) chooses an effort level considering both the disutility from effort and the expected utility from earnings under the compensation plan. The Agency Theory framework provides an explanation for the differences across firms in the types of compensation plans used, such as straight salary, straight commissions, or a combination of salary and commissions. It is shown that the optimal compensation plan is a convex (concave) increasing function of sales if the risk tolerance of the salesperson increases "rapidly" (stays constant) with income. We identify several structural parameters that affect the compensation plan and show that the implication of changes in some of these parameters is consistent with those mentioned in the sales management literature. For example, we show that the proportion of salary to total compensation would increase with an increase in one or more of the following parameters: (i) uncertainty, (ii) marginal cost of production, and (iii) attractiveness of alternative job opportunities for the salesperson. We conclude with a discussion of the implications of the theory for managing salesforce compensation plans.

Buell, Victor P.
The Changing Role of the Product Manager in Consumer Goods Companies
Journal of Marketing 39 (3) (July 1975), 3–11.
1975 Alpha Kappa Psi Award Winner (as of 1996, the Marketing Science Institute H. Paul Root Award)

The role of the product manager in consumer goods companies continues to be controversial, particularly with respect to the management of advertising. This study, made among top and middle managers in companies that lead the nation in advertising expenditures, shows how these companies are attempting to strengthen the planning and coordination functions of product managers while restricting their authority to make decisions.

Churchill, Gilbert A., Jr., Neil M. Ford, and Orville C. Walker, Jr.
Organizational Climate and Job Satisfaction in the Salesforce
Journal of Marketing Research 13 (4) (November 1976), 323–32.
Co-winner of the 1981 William F. O'Dell Award

This report concerns the impact of several organizational climate variables on the job satisfaction of a cross-section of industrial salesmen. To gain greater insight into how climate affects salesmen's feelings about their jobs, the relationships between each climate variable and each of seven components of job satisfaction also are examined. Finally, the managerial implications of the findings are explored, and actions that might lead to improvements in salesforce morale are discussed.

Day, George S.
The Capabilities of Market-Driven Organizations
Journal of Marketing 58 (4) (October 1994), 37–52.
1994 Harold H. Maynard Award Winner and 2003 Sheth Foundation/*Journal of Marketing* Award Winner

Considerable progress has been made in identifying market-driven businesses, understanding what they do, and measuring the bottom-line consequences of their orientation to their markets. The next challenge is to understand how this organizational orientation can be achieved and sustained. The emerging capabilities approach to strategic management, when coupled with total quality management, offers a rich array of ways to design change programs that will enhance a market orientation. The most distinctive features of market-driven organizations are their mastery of the market sensing and customer linking capabilities. A comprehensive change program aimed at enhancing these capabilities includes: (1) the diagnosis of current capabilities, (2) anticipation of future needs for capabilities, (3) bottom-up redesign of underlying processes, (4) top-down direction and commitment, (5) creative use of information technology, and (5) continuous monitoring of progress.

Goodman, Charles S.
Do the Poor Pay More?
Journal of Marketing 32 (1) (January 1968),18–24.
1968 Alpha Kappa Psi Award Winner (as of 1996, the Marketing Science Institute H. Paul Root Award)

Are low-income families victims of high prices in small neighborhood stores? This article goes beyond asking what prices small stores charge and examines the purchasing patterns of low-income families. What kind of stores do they patronize? Why? Do they use the convenience stores in the low-income areas? Do many buy food on credit? How well do they perceive price differences among stores? These are some of the questions answered through a survey in a Philadelphia redevelopment area.

Grether, E. T.
Marketing and Public Policy: A Contemporary View
Journal of Marketing 38 (3) (July 1974), 2–7.
1974 Alpha Kappa Psi Award Winner (as of 1996, the Marketing Science Institute H. Paul Root Award)

The national economic policy intended to maintain competition is rooted in classical partial equilibrium analysis, usually with about a 25-year cultural lag between economic analysis and law and regulation. In this article, E. T. Grether examines the market structure analysis approach in relation to both the enforcement of the national economic policy of competition and the recent and current ecological-social, environmental-holistic urgencies. Looking ahead—what is the solid ground for marketing scholars and practitioners to observe, interpret, or participate in the market action?

Grether, E. T., and Robert J. Holloway

Impact of Government upon the Market System

Journal of Marketing 31 (2) (April 1967), 1–5.

1967 Alpha Kappa Psi Award Winner (as of 1996, the Marketing Science Institute H. Paul Root Award)

Suggestions are presented for research on the impact of governmental policies, programs, and regulations upon the functioning of the market system as a whole, and upon specific subsystems. The authors point out that intervention by government at all levels is one of the two most significant environmental forces affecting marketing. This paper is the first of four reports developed by the AMA Task Force on Research on Basic Problems in Marketing, chaired by Donald R. Longman. The other papers will be presented in subsequent issues of the *Journal of Marketing*. Each paper will be accompanied by a review by Seymour Banks, in which the issues involved in each paper will be highlighted and the various papers related to one another.

Hunt, Shelby D.

The Nature and Scope of Marketing

Journal of Marketing 40 (3) (July 1976), 17–28.

1976 Harold H. Maynard Award Winner

Can a new model of the scope of marketing help resolve the "nature of marketing" and "marketing science" controversies?

Hunt, Shelby D.

General Theories and the Fundamental Explananda of Marketing

Journal of Marketing 47 (4) (Fall 1983), 9–17.

1983 Harold H. Maynard Award Winner

Is a general theory of marketing possible? If so, what would it look like? This article (1) briefly examines the nature of theory in marketing, (2) explores the characteristics of general theories in the philosophy of science, (3) proposes what a general theory of marketing would attempt to explain and predict, (4) delineates the structure of general theories, both in and of marketing, and (5) evaluates the status of general theories in/of marketing.

Jaworski, Bernard J., and Ajay K. Kohli

Market Orientation: Antecedents and Consequences

Journal of Marketing 57 (3) (July 1993), 53–70.

2001 Sheth Foundation/*Journal of Marketing* Award Winner

This research addresses three questions: (1) Why are some organizations more market-oriented than others? (2) What effect does a market orientation have on employees and business perform-ance? (3) Does the linkage between a market orientation and business performance depend on the environmental context? The findings from two national samples suggest that a market orienta-tion is related to top management emphasis on the orientation, risk aversion of top managers, inter-departmental conflict and connectedness, centralization, and reward system orientation. Furthermore, the findings suggest that a market orientation is related to overall (judgmental) busi-ness performance (but not market share), employees' organizational commitment, and esprit de corps. Finally, the linkage between a market orientation and performance appears to be robust across environmental contexts that are characterized by varying degrees of market turbulence, competitive intensity, and technological turbulence.

Kohli, Ajay K., and Bernard J. Jaworski

Market Orientation: The Construct, Research Propositions, and Managerial Implications

Journal of Marketing 54 (2) (April 1990), 1–18.

1990 Alpha Kappa Psi Award Winner (as of 1996, the Marketing Science Institute H. Paul Root Award)

The literature reflects remarkably little effort to develop a framework for understanding the imple-mentation of the marketing concept. The authors synthesize extant knowledge on the subject and provide a foundation for future research by clarifying the construct's domain, developing research propositions, and constructing an integrating framework that includes antecedents and conse-quences of a market orientation. They draw on the occasional writings on the subject over the last 35 years in the marketing literature, work in related disciplines, and 62 field interviews with man-agers in diverse functions and organizations. Managerial implications of this research are discussed.

Kotler, Philip
A Generic Concept of Marketing
Journal of Marketing 36 (2) (April 1972), 46–54.
1972 Alpha Kappa Psi Award Winner (as of 1996, the Marketing Science Institute H. Paul Root Award)

The proposal that marketing is relevant to all organizations having customer groups was advanced in the January, 1969 issue of this journal. It is now stated that the original broadening proposal should be broadened still further to include the transactions between an organization and all of its publics. The author sees marketing as the disciplined task of creating and offering values to others for the purpose of achieving a desired response. The generic view of marketing is defined by a set of four axioms and leads to new marketing typologies and views of the tasks of marketing management.

Kotler, Philip, and Sidney J. Levy
Broadening the Concept of Marketing
Journal of Marketing 33 (1) (January 1969), 10–5.
1969 Alpha Kappa Psi Award Winner (as of 1996, the Marketing Science Institute H. Paul Root Award)

Marketing is a pervasive societal activity that goes considerably beyond the selling of toothpaste, soap, and steel. The authors interpret the meaning of marketing for nonbusiness organizations and the nature of marketing functions such as product improvement, pricing, distribution, and communication in such organizations. The question considered is whether traditional marketing principles are transferable to the marketing of organizations, persons, and ideas.

Kotler, Philip, and Gerald Zaltman
Social Marketing: An Approach to Planned Social Change
Journal of Marketing 35 (3) (July 1971), 3–12.
1971 Alpha Kappa Psi Award Winner (as of 1996, the Marketing Science Institute H. Paul Root Award)

Can marketing concepts and techniques be effectively applied to the promotion of social objectives such as brotherhood, safe driving, and family planning? The applicability of marketing concepts to such social problems is examined in this article. The authors show how social causes can be advanced more successfully through applying principles of marketing analysis, planning, and control to problems of social change.

Leighton, David S. R.

The Internationalization of American Business: The Third Industrial Revolution

Journal of Marketing 34 (3) (July 1970), 3–6.

1970 Alpha Kappa Psi Award Winner (as of 1996, the Marketing Science Institute H. Paul Root Award)

The revolution in management techniques of the last 15 years has spurred the growth of large international companies of a complexity hitherto unknown. A complete rethinking of traditional views of trade is required.

Leone, Robert P., and Randall L. Schultz

A Study of Marketing Generalizations

Journal of Marketing 44 (1) (Winter 1980), 10–8.

Co-winner of the 1980 Harold H. Maynard Award

This paper deals with what is known as opposed to what is thought about marketing. The distinction is not subtle. The knowledge of a field is defined in terms of scientific generalizations, whereas theory or thought is necessarily speculative. We argue that marketing generalizations logically precede marketing theories and that marketing generalizations are marketing knowledge.

Menon, Anil, Sundar G. Bharadwaj, Phani Tej Adidam, and Steven W. Edison

Antecedents and Consequences of Marketing Strategy Making: A Model and a Test

Journal of Marketing 63 (2) (April 1999), 18–40.

Co-winner of the 1999 Marketing Science Institute H. Paul Root Award

There is a strong rekindling of academic and practitioner interest in the marketing strategy making (MSM) process and its effect on firm performance. However, there is a dearth of research on process issues in marketing strategy. This study attempts to fill this important gap in the marketing strategy literature by using a discovery-oriented approach to develop a (1) multifaceted conceptualization of MSM, (2) model of the antecedents and consequences of MSM, and (3) test of this model using data on more than 200 marketing mix-related decisions. After ruling out common method bias, the authors find that innovative culture is the fundamental antecedent of effective MSM. They also find that the components of MSM (situation analysis, comprehensiveness, emphasis on marketing assets and capabilities, cross-functional integration, communication quality, consensus commitment, and resource commitment) have differential effects on the outcomes measured, strategy creativity, organizational learning, and market performance. The authors find that strategy creativity affects market performance and organizational learning directly and as a mediator variable.

Tucker, W. T.

Future Directions in Marketing Theory

Journal of Marketing 38 (2) (April 1974), 30–35.

1974 Harold H. Maynard Award Winner

Marketing theory generally has related to a well-defined set of structures and processes and has maintained a relatively consistent point of view. This article analyzes current pressures to change the definition of marketing and discusses two possible viewpoints that could aid in the development of consonant theory.

Varadarajan, P. Rajan, Satish Jayachandran, and J. Chris White

Strategic Interdependence in Organizations: Deconglomeration and Marketing Strategy

Journal of Marketing 65 (1) (January 2001), 15–28.

2001 Harold H. Maynard Award Winner

Although strategy exists at multiple levels in a firm (corporate, business, and functional), there is a dearth of research in marketing literature that focuses on the dependency among strategy at different levels. The authors address this issue by examining the relationship between deconglomeration and marketing strategy. Deconglomeration refers to the divestiture behavior of a conglomerate firm and the transformation of its business portfolio from one that is largely composed of several unrelated businesses to one composed of fewer and related businesses.

Drawing on multiple theoretical perspectives, the authors propose a conceptual model delineating the environmental and organizational drivers of deconglomeration and its outcomes for marketing. The authors suggest that after deconglomeration, (1) a firm can be expected to be more competitor and customer oriented, (2) multimarket contact with competing firms and seller concentration will increase, (3) businesses retained by the firm will be more innovative and place greater emphasis on advertising compared with sales promotion, and (4) the firm's culture may become more externally oriented. Furthermore, the locus of decision making for marketing strategy may shift more toward senior management levels. In summary, changes in a firm's corporate strategy could lead to significant changes in the marketing strategy of its business units.

Vargo, Stephen L., and Robert F. Lusch

Evolving to a New Dominant Logic for Marketing

Journal of Marketing 68 (1) (January 2004), 1–17.

2004 Harold H. Maynard Award Winner

Marketing inherited a model of exchange from economics, which had a dominant logic based on the exchange of "goods," which usually are manufactured output. The dominant logic focused on tangible resources, embedded value, and transactions. Over the past several decades, new perspectives have emerged that have a revised logic focused on intangible resources, the cocreation of value, and relationships. The authors believe that the new perspectives are converging to form a new dominant logic for marketing, one in which service provision rather than goods is fundamental to economic exchange. The authors explore this evolving logic and the corresponding shift in perspective for marketing scholars, marketing practitioners, and marketing educators.

Walker, Orville C., Jr., and Robert W. Ruekert

Marketing's Role in the Implementation of Business Strategies: A Critical Review and Conceptual Framework

Journal of Marketing 51 (3) (July 1987), 15–33.

1987 Harold H. Maynard Award Winner

The authors review and integrate various theoretical perspectives, normative statements, and pieces of empirical evidence about the organizational structures and processes best suited for implementing different types of business strategies. Particular emphasis is given to the relationship of different types of structure, processes, and policies involved in the performance of marketing activities to the overall performance of different business strategies. Several specific research propositions are developed.

Webster, Frederick E., Jr.

The Changing Role of Marketing in the Corporation

Journal of Marketing 56 (4) (October 1992), 1–17.

1992 Alpha Kappa Psi Award Winner (as of 1996, the Marketing Science Institute H. Paul Root Award)

An earlier version of this paper appeared as MSI Report No. 91–127.

New organization forms, including strategic partnerships and networks, are replacing simple market-based transactions and traditional bureaucratic hierarchical organizations. The historical marketing management function, based on the microeconomic maximization paradigm, must be critically examined for its relevance to marketing theory and practice in the 1990s. A new conception of marketing will focus on managing strategic partnerships and positioning the firm between vendors and customers in the value chain with the aim of delivering superior value to customers. Customer relationships will be seen as the key strategic resource of the business.

Additional Relevant Papers: The Role of Marketing

Firat, A. Fuat, and Alladi Venkatesh
Liberatory Postmodernism and the Reenchantment of Consumption
Journal of Consumer Research 22 (3) (December 1995), 239–67. See page 92 for abstract.
1998 *Journal of Consumer Research* Best Article Award Winner

Friestad, Marian, and Peter Wright
The Persuasion Knowledge Model: How People Cope with Persuasion Attempts
Journal of Consumer Research 21 (1) (June 1994), 1–31. See page 120 for abstract.
1997 *Journal of Consumer Research* Best Article Award Winner

Gardner, David M.
Deception in Advertising: A Conceptual Approach
Journal of Marketing 39 (1) (January 1975), 40–6. See page 120 for abstract.
1975 Harold H. Maynard Award Winner

Glazer, Rashi
Marketing in an Information-Intensive Environment: Strategic Implications of Knowledge as an Asset
Journal of Marketing 55 (4) (October 1991), 1–19. See page 177 for abstract.
1991 Harold H. Maynard Award Winner

Green, Paul E.
Bayesian Decision Theory in Pricing Strategy
Journal of Marketing 27 (1) (January 1963), 5–14. See page 93 for abstract.
Co-winner of the 1963 Alpha Kappa Psi Award (as of 1996, the Marketing Science Institute H. Paul Root Award)

Hunt, Shelby D., and Robert M. Morgan
The Comparative Advantage Theory of Competition
Journal of Marketing 59 (2) (April 1995), 1–15. See page 179 for abstract.
1995 Harold H. Maynard Award Winner

Martineau, Pierre
Social Classes and Spending Behavior
Journal of Marketing 23 (2) (October 1958), 121–30. See page 156 for abstract.
1958 Alpha Kappa Psi Award Winner (as of 1996, the Marketing Science Institute H. Paul Root Award)

McCracken, Grant
Culture and Consumption: A Theoretical Account of the Structure and Movement of the Cultural Meaning of Consumer Goods
Journal of Consumer Research 13 (1) (June 1986), 71–84. See page 156 for abstract.
1987 Association for Consumer Research Best Article Award Winner (as of 1996, *Journal of Consumer Research* Best Article Award)

Mitra, Anusree, and John G. Lynch, Jr.
Toward a Reconciliation of Market Power and Information Theories of Advertising Effects on Price Elasticity
Journal of Consumer Research 21 (4) (March 1995), 644–59. See page 125 for abstract.
1995 Robert Ferber Award Winner

Moore, Elizabeth S., and Richard J. Lutz
Children, Advertising, and Product Experiences: A Multimethod Inquiry
Journal of Consumer Research 26 (1) (June 2000), 31–48. See page 125 for abstract.
Co-winner of the 2003 *Journal of Consumer Research* Best Article Award

O'Guinn, Thomas C., and L. J. Shrum
The Role of Television in the Construction of Consumer Reality
Journal of Consumer Research 23 (4) (March 1997), 278–94. See page 129 for abstract.
Co-winner of the 2000 *Journal of Consumer Research* Best Article Award

Pechmann, Cornelia, and Susan J. Knight

An Experimental Investigation of the Joint Effects of Advertising and Peers on Adolescents' Beliefs and Intentions about Cigarette Smoking

Journal of Consumer Research 29 (1) (June 2002), 5–19. See page 130 for abstract.

2005 *Journal of Consumer Research* Best Article Award

Roberts, Harry V.

Bayesian Statistics in Marketing

Journal of Marketing 27 (1) (January 1963), 1–4. See page 99 for abstract.

Co-winner of the 1963 Alpha Kappa Psi Award (as of 1996, the Marketing Science Institute H. Paul Root Award)

Smith, Wendell R.

Product Differentiation and Market Segmentation as Alternative Marketing Strategies

Journal of Marketing 21 (1) (July 1956), 3–8. See page 185 for abstract.

1956 Alpha Kappa Psi Award Winner (as of 1996, the Marketing Science Institute H. Paul Root Award)

White, Irving S.

The Functions of Advertising in Our Culture

Journal of Marketing 24 (1) (July 1959), 8–14. See page 134 for abstract.

1959 Alpha Kappa Psi Award Winner (as of 1996, the Marketing Science Institute H. Paul Root Award)

6

Research Tools

In the earliest of the prize-winning papers on research tools in marketing, Ferber (1955) argued for going beyond econometric models based on national-level government statistics (e.g., changes in income) to forecast a brand's sales. He suggested that a marketer could build a forecast from a survey completed by a representative sample of potential buyers regarding their attitudes, plans, and purchase intentions. In other early work, Buzzell and Slater (1962), Roberts (1963), and Green (1963) showed how decision theory and Bayesian statistics could help managers make marketing decisions.

After a few decades of tool development in the field, Little (1979) proposed the coordination of the many kinds of data, systems, tools, and techniques then available into a "marketing decision support system." Little went on to predict that the looming explosion of data and computer power were going to shift the focus of marketing research from status reports, such as Ferber's survey-based sales forecast, to response reports that allow marketers to uncover the relationship between their marketing activity and the sales that are likely to occur. Choffray and Lilien (1978) provided such a model for industrial marketers. Their four submodels of the industrial buying center can be parameterized with existing data, additional survey data, and managerial judgment to provide a forecasting and diagnostic tool. Wind (1973) combined conjoint analysis and multidimensional scaling to suggest a new method for concept testing.

Green, Carroll, and Goldberg (1981) applied conjoint analysis to the problem of optimal product design by using utility functions from conjoint analysis to build a choice simulator. Market share results from the choice simulator are linked back to product attributes to create a response surface describing market response to all possible attribute combinations.

We cover the remaining prize-winning papers in sections on the development of important marketing research tools: conjoint analysis, choice models, market structure and segmentation methodologies, other quantitative tools, and qualitative tools.

Conjoint Analysis

Conjoint analysis is a technique for transforming a subject's rank ordering of product profiles (where product profiles are products described by their values on a set of attributes) into a utility function that reports the relative importance that different product attributes have for that subject. Johnson (1974) extended conjoint analysis by proposing that subjects be asked to consider only two attributes at a time and to report the way they would make tradeoffs between different levels of those two attributes. Perreault and Young (1980) presented Alternating Least Squares analysis as a method to estimate utility functions from ordinal data such as rank orderings of product profiles, while simultaneously converting that ordinal data into interval-scaled data. Green (1984) simplified the response task in conjoint analysis by combining self-explication (self-reports of attribute-level desirability and attribute importance weights) with response to a limited set of product profiles to yield hybrid conjoint analysis.

More recently, Toubia et al. (2003) exploited new developments in math programming to produce an algorithm for designing and estimating adaptive questions for conjoint analysis with partial product profiles. After a subject gives initial feedback regarding product preferences, the algorithm is able to quickly search the parameter space and, in real time, design the next question in a way that will resolve the largest amount of the remaining uncertainty about the subject's utility function.

Glazer (1984) addressed the problem of conjoint analysis's assumption of independence between how valuable consumers perceive particular attributes to be and their preferences for different choice options. Earlier research had shown that consumers perceive the attributes in choice options they prefer to be more valuable than the attributes in choice options they do not prefer—a so-called halo effect. Glazer presented a model that quantified the extent to which choice preferences influence perceptions of attribute value.

Finally, Lynch (1985) presents methods that can be used to determine whether a subject's utility function is additive, multiplicative, or multilinear. He describes the kinds of evidence and experimental designs that would allow one to distinguish among the alternative model forms.

Choice Models

Hauser and Wisniewski (1982) presented a dynamic stochastic model of consumers' response to a new transportation service and to that new service's marketing activities. The simple model, estimated using survey data, helped a manager make a better decision. Currim (1982), also concerned with forecasting consumers' response to a new transportation service, proposed a modification of logit and probit models. Those models' assumption of the "independence of irrelevant alternatives" dictates that a new service option must take sales from existing options in proportion to those existing options' current market shares. Currim's extension relaxes that assumption. Fader and Hardie (1996) combined the ability of conjoint analysis to include a wide range of choice options with the ability of choice models to derive utility functions from observed choices. Defining each choice alternative by its value on a set of attributes, Fader and Hardie used choice model technology to estimate attribute importance weights rather than to estimate brand-specific constants.

Jain and Vilcassim (1991), who focused on the purchase-timing decision, provided a generalized version of the proportional-hazard model that enabled researchers to choose among purchase-timing models (negative binomial, Erlang family, Erlang 2, inverse Gaussian, lognormal, exponential) while accounting for the effects of marketing mix and unobserved heterogeneity.

Erdem and Keane (1996) extended choice models to account for shifts in market response parameters that are driven by changes in the marketing environment. Traditional reduced-form analysis does not take into account the fact that consumers' choice behavior may be influenced by marketing policy, whereas Erdem and Keane's application of structural analysis made it possible to consider the marketplace implications of changes in marketing policy.

Market Structure and Segmentation

In this section, we group together market structure models and segmentation models, because the two kinds of analyses can be closely linked. We first describe two market-structure-only models, then describe a model that links market structure and segmentation, and conclude with two models that link segmentation analysis to positioning.

In reaction to models of market structure that used hierarchical clustering (which requires exclusive group membership) to group competitive brands together, Srivastava, Alpert, and Shocker (1984) asked customers to judge the appropriateness of each of 24 services for each of 12 usage situations and analyzed the data with a clustering algorithm that allows clusters to overlap. They showed that when defining market structure for alternatives with multiple uses, overlapping clusters provide more managerial insight. Focusing on a narrower range of brands, Allenby (1989) presented an iterative methodology based on scanner data to infer market structure while refining estimates of cross-elasticities. The procedure begins by estimating $n(n - 1)$ cross-elasticities for the n brands in a product category. Those preliminary estimates define a two-dimensional map of interbrand distances from which one can infer a first estimate of the number of submarkets (s) and the brands included in each submarket. Exploiting the submarket structure reduces the number of cross-elasticities estimated on the next iteration from $n(n - 1)$ to $2s$.

Grover and Srinivasan (1987) used latent-class analysis to identify customer segments and then identify market structure by defining brands as competitors if they have high choice probability in a particular customer segment. Like Srivastava, Alpert, and Shocker's overlapping cluster methodology, Grover and Srinivasan's latent-class methodology can represent a brand as competing in more than one submarket.

Green and Krieger (1991) compared approaches to segmentation based on the output of conjoint analysis (e.g., cluster on attribute importance weights or cluster on attribute-level desirabilities or part-worths) and showed how those different approaches lead to different positioning for potential new products. Ter Hofstede, Steenkamp, and Wedel (1999) also linked segmentation and positioning by forming segments based on means-end chains. Their method identifies segments that cross national boundaries and allows for heterogeneity in response behavior within and across countries. Their model yields a probabilistic classification of consumers rather than the deterministic classification resulting from K-means clustering. This probabilistic classification represents a flexibility for segmentation analysis that is analogous to the flexibility for market structure analysis provided by Srivastava, Alpert, and Shocker's overlapping clusters and Grover and Srinivasan's latent-class analysis.

Other Quantitative Tools

Wells (1975) began his review of psychographic research with the observation that demographic descriptions had become inadequate. Psychographic research, growing out of two streams of research (personality inventories and clinical psychology's small-scale "qualitative study"), had taken on at least five different forms. Wells pointed out that psychographic variables are useful: they tend to relate to one another, to demographics, and to the use of products and media. Though he acknowledged that there was work to be done on the construct validity of those variables, he predicted that psychographic methods would become a part of mainstream marketing research.

Peter (1981) focused the field on the importance of construct validity. Reviewing the 12 construct validation studies published in the *Journal of Marketing Research* between 1973 and 1979, he found seven with some support for convergent validity, five with some support for discriminant validity, and five with some support for nomological validity. He concluded that few, if any, measures could meet rigorous construct validation criteria in a series of studies.

Bagozzi (1977) derived and illustrated structural equation modeling for the analysis of experiments; he also pointed out that the technology could be applied to survey research, panel studies, and longitudinal research.

Hoffman and Franke (1986) introduced correspondence analysis to the field of marketing. This exploratory data analysis tool is similar to principal-components analysis, canonical correlation analysis, and discriminant analysis. It differs from those techniques in that it quantifies multivariate categorical data.

Bronnenberg and Sismeiro (2002) provided a spatial methodology for inferring missing data. Applied to multimarket scanner data, the methodology allows one to predict brand performance in markets for which no data are available. It performs better than global-market averages, nearest-neighbor predictions, or local averages and draws estimates toward their local averages.

Qualitative Tools

Levy (1981) described verbal material from consumers in the marketplace (e.g., focus group interviews, depth interviews) as a form of storytelling that could be analyzed with tools from clinical psychology, social anthropology, and/or literary criticism. He encouraged further study of the development of families' "little myths," the evolution of common cultural "little myths," the way facts of behavior are changed when reported, and how advertisers participate in creating symbolic vocabulary and use consumers' myths on behalf of their products.

Mick (1986) gave examples of how semiotics could be used to study the semantic properties of advertising messages, the communicational properties of women's clothing, and the evolving perceptions of owned products as new products and styles emerge. He encouraged consumer behavior researchers to explore semiotics as a route to new insights.

Firat and Venkatesh (1995) critiqued modernism (the philosophical and sociocultural ideas characteristic of Western history from the late 16th or early 17th century until the late 20th century). Among the points they made were that "modern" is defined by science, rationalism, and technology, while "postmodern" also includes culture (aesthetics, language, discourse, practices). They argued that modernism failed to produce an ethical, rational, technology-oriented unifying social order, that modernism reduced the world to dichotomies (subject/object, male/female, producer/consumer), and that with modernism there is little connection between the ideal and reality. In a postmodernist approach to marketing, a consumer should not be seen as a person seeking to satisfy a need, but rather as a person seeking to produce symbols; each willing consumer can be an equal participant in the production (construction) of self. Postmodernism does not advocate the abandonment of scientific procedures, but it holds that scientific knowledge is not the only kind of knowledge.

Research Priorities

MSI corporate members are asking for new, non-traditional tools and methods for developing a proactive understanding of the consumer (e.g., anthropology, web-based surveys, scenario analysis) and for validation of those tools and methods. They want to understand the processes needed to ensure the adoption and use of new tools and methodologies and to ensure customer-relevant innovation in all stages of new product/service development. They want to understand the role of marketing research in discontinuous innovation. These practitioners need better methods for predicting new product/service adoption and for assessing the effectiveness of the new product development process. This group wants to know how to measure brand equity, how to relate brand and customer equity, how marketing programs impact brand and customer equity, and how the impact of marketing programs changes over the product life cycle.

Abstracts: Research Tools

Allenby, Greg M.

A Unified Approach to Identifying, Estimating and Testing Demand Structures with Aggregate Scanner Data

Marketing Science 8 (3) (Summer 1989), 265–80.

1990 Frank M. Bass Dissertation Paper Award Winner

A one-to-one map between a specific demand structure and a restricted cross-elasticity matrix is developed and tested using a random utility model. The resulting demand structure can be used to evaluate a firm's ability to differentiate its products, and can help determine if demand is characterized by factors that are easy to change. Similar brands are assumed to share common attributes that are stochastically evaluated by the consumer, resulting in a random utility model with correlated errors. The map results in more precise cross-elasticity estimates and can be used to both identify and test possible structures.

Bagozzi, Richard P.

Structural Equation Models in Experimental Research

Journal of Marketing Research 14 (2) (May 1977), 209–26.

1982 William F. O'Dell Award Winner

A general model is derived and illustrated for the analysis of field and laboratory experimental data. The model explicitly provides for the determination of the magnitude and significance of experimental effects and can be used in a diagnostic sense in the interpretation and design of experiments. Comparisons are made with the analysis of variance technique where applicable.

Bronnenberg, Bart J., and Catarina Sismeiro

Using Multimarket Data to Predict Brand Performance in Markets for Which No or Poor Data Exist

Journal of Marketing Research 39 (1) (February 2002), 1–17.

2003 Paul E. Green Award Winner

The authors show how multimarket data can be used to make predictions about brand performance in markets for which no or poor data exist. To obtain these predictions, the authors propose a model for market similarity that incorporates the structure of the U.S. retailing industry and the geographic location of markets. The model makes use of the idea that if two markets have the same retailers or are located close to each other, then branded goods in these markets should have similar sales performance (other factors being held constant). In holdout samples, the proposed spatial prediction method improves greatly on naive predictors such as global-market averages, nearest neighbor predictors, or local averages. In addition, the authors show that the spatial model gives more plausible estimates of price elasticities. It does so for two reasons. First, the spatial model helps solve an omitted variables problem by allowing for unobserved factors with a cross-market structure. An example of such unobserved factors is the shelf-space allocations made at the retail-chain level. Second, the model deals with uninformative estimates of price elasticities by drawing them toward their local averages. The authors discuss other substantive issues as well as future research.

Buzzell, Robert D., and Charles C. Slater

Decision Theory and Marketing Management

Journal of Marketing 26 (3) (July 1962), 7–16.

1962 Alpha Kappa Psi Award Winner (as of 1996, the Marketing Science Institute H. Paul Root Award)

The article discusses three topics: a brief summary of decision theory as a tool of marketing management; a description of the nature and sources of wholesale bakers' present marketing problems; and a step-by-step account of the use of decision theory in the analysis of one of these problems.

Choffray, Jean-Marie, and Gary L. Lilien

Assessing Response to Industrial Marketing Strategy

Journal of Marketing 42 (2) (April 1978), 20–31.

1978 Alpha Kappa Psi Award Winner (as of 1996, the Marketing Science Institute H. Paul Root Award)

An operational model that can be used for developing strategy for product design, positioning, and market communications.

Currim, Imran S.

Predictive Testing of Consumer Choice Models Not Subject to Independence of Irrelevant Alternatives

Journal of Marketing Research 19 (2) (May 1982), 208–22.

1987 William F. O'Dell Award Winner

The probabilistic modeling of the relationship between objective or perceived characteristics of multiattribute alternatives and consumer choice is receiving increased attention in marketing and other disciplines. Many marketing applications use the Luce choice axiom, the LOGIT model, and the independent PROBIT model. All these formulations involve the "independence of irrelevant alternatives" assumption, which is not realistic in many consumer behavior contexts. The author suggests new product introduction situations in which the consequences of the assumption are not intuitively appealing. Models recently developed by transportation researchers and one extension developed by the author, all of which are not constrained by the independence restriction and may be applicable in modeling consumer choice, are described. In an empirical application, cross-sectional data on consumers' perceptions of transportation modes on several characteristics and their choices of modes in the San Francisco Bay area are used to compare models with and without the independence property on diagnostic and predictive criteria.

Erdem, Tulin, and Michael P. Keane

Decision-Making under Uncertainty: Capturing Dynamic Brand Choice Processes in Turbulent Consumer Goods Markets

Marketing Science 15 (1) (Winter 1996), 1–20.

1996 Frank M. Bass Dissertation Paper Award Winner and 1996 John D. C. Little Award Winner

We construct two models of the behavior of consumers in an environment where there is uncertainty about brand attributes. In our models, both usage experience and advertising exposure give consumers noisy signals about brand attributes. Consumers use these signals to update their expectations of brand attributes in a Bayesian manner. The two models are (1) a dynamic model with immediate utility maximization, and (2) a dynamic "forward-looking" model in which consumers maximize the expected present value of utility over a planning horizon. Given this theoretical framework, we derive from the Bayesian learning framework how brand choice probabilities depend on past usage experience and advertising exposures. We then form likelihood functions for the models and estimate them on Nielsen scanner data for detergent.

We find that the functional forms for experience and advertising effects that we derive from the Bayesian learning framework fit the data very well relative to flexible ad hoc functional forms such as exponential smoothing, and also perform better at out-of-sample prediction. Another finding is that in the context of consumer learning of product attributes, although the forward-looking model fits the data statistically better at conventional significance levels, both models produce similar parameter estimates and policy implications. Our estimates indicate that consumers are risk-averse with respect to variation in brand attributes, which discourages them from buying unfamiliar brands. Using the estimated behavioral models, we perform various scenario evaluations to find how changes in marketing strategy affect brand choice both in the short and long run. A key finding obtained from the policy experiments is that advertising intensity has only weak short run effects, but a strong cumulative effect in the long run. The substantive content of the paper is potentially of interest to academics in marketing, economics and decision sciences, as well as product managers, marketing research managers and analysts interested in studying the effectiveness of marketing mix strategies. Our paper will be of particular interest to those interested in the long run effects of advertising.

Note that our estimation strategy requires us to specify explicit behavioral models of consumer choice behavior, derive the implied relationships among choice probabilities, past purchases and marketing mix variables, and then estimate the behavioral parameters of each model. Such an estimation strategy is referred to as "structural" estimation, and econometric models that are based explicitly on the consumer's maximization problem and whose parameters are parameters of the consumers' utility functions or of their constraints are referred to as "structural" models. A key benefit of the structural approach is its potential usefulness for policy evaluation. The parameters of structural models are invariant to policy, that is, they do not change due to a change in the policy. In contrast, the parameters of reduced form brand choice models are, in general, functions of marketing strategy variables (e.g., consumer response to price may depend on pricing policy). As a result, the predictions of reduced form models for the outcomes of policy experiments may be unreliable, because in making the prediction one must assume that the model parameters are unaffected by the policy change.

Since the agents in our models choose among many alternative brands, their choice probabilities take the form of higher-order integrals.

We employ Monte Carlo methods to approximate these integrals and estimate our models using simulated maximum likelihood. Estimation of the dynamic forward-looking model also requires that a dynamic programming problem be solved in order to form the likelihood function. For this we use a new approximation method based on simulation and interpolation techniques. These estimation techniques may be of interest to researchers and policy makers in many fields where dynamic choice among discrete alternatives is important, such as marketing, decision sciences, labor and health economics, and industrial organization.

Fader, Peter S., and Bruce G. S. Hardie
Modeling Consumer Choice among SKUs
Journal of Marketing Research 33 (4) (November 1996), 442–52.
1997 Paul E. Green Award Winner

Most choice models in marketing implicitly assume that the fundamental unit of analysis is the brand. In reality, however, many more of the decisions made by consumers, manufacturers, and retailers occur at the level of the stock-keeping unit (SKU). The authors address a variety of issues involved in defining and using SKUs in a choice model, as well as the unique benefits that arise from doing so. They discuss how a set of discrete attributes (e.g., brand name, package size, type) can be used to characterize a large set of SKUs in a parsimonious manner. They postulate that consumers do not form preferences for each individual SKU, per se, but instead evaluate the underlying attributes that describe each item. The model is shown to be substantially superior to a more traditional framework that does not emphasize the complete use of SKU attribute information. Their analysis also highlights several other benefits associated with the proposed modeling approach, such as the ability to forecast sales for imitative line extensions that enter the market in a future period. Other implications and extensions also are discussed.

Ferber, Robert
Sales Forecasting by Sample Surveys
Journal of Marketing 20 (1) (July 1955), 1–13.
1955 Alpha Kappa Psi Award Winner (as of 1996, the Marketing Science Institute H. Paul Root Award)

The use of sample surveys to forecast sales is still in its infancy. Sampling is undoubtedly one of the most expensive means of consumer goods sales forecasting because it invariably is carried out by personal interviews. Proponents of sampling might well argue that the costs of sampling are negligible compared with the amounts at stake. Nevertheless the fact remains that few small consumer goods companies are likely to be willing to incur those costs when alternative methods are so much more economical and when there is no assurance of the superiority of the sampling approach. Sampling differs radically in a number of important respects from other methods of sales forecasting, and differences must be considered carefully in determining whether the method is feasible for any given case. Nevertheless, the general nature of the problem is sufficiently similar to warrant a few broad generalizations. These generalizations relate to a number of the more important aspects of the problem, but by no means do they refer to all of them.

Firat, A. Fuat, and Alladi Venkatesh
Liberatory Postmodernism and the Reenchantment of Consumption
Journal of Consumer Research 22 (3) (December 1995), 239–67.
1998 *Journal of Consumer Research* Best Article Award Winner

In this article, we elaborate on various key ideas about consumption and consumers from a theoretical position that we have labeled "liberatory postmodernism." By unmasking the limitations of modernism that have to do with the onerous nature of its metanarratives and narrow conventionalism, we show that postmodern developments offer alternate visions of consumption processes that have an emancipatory potential. The analysis in our article begins with a discussion of the philosophical foundations of modernism and postmodernism followed by a cultural critique of modernism—exposing, for example, the modernist distinction between production and consumption and the privileging of production over consumption. We demonstrate how postmodernism is concerned with the reversing of the conditions of modernity and with a wide range of issues regarding the construction of the subject (i.e., the consumer), the role of the symbolic in consumption processes, the notion of the spectacularization of life, the creation of the hyperreal, and the cultural signification of fragmentation. We conclude the article with a proposal for an epistemology of consumption that subsumes scientific knowledge under a broader category of narrative knowledge and recognizes multivocality of consumption forms.

Glazer, Rashi

Multiattribute Perceptual Bias as Revealing of Preference Structure

Journal of Consumer Research 11 (1) (June 1984), 510–21.

1982 Robert Ferber Award Winner

The assumed separation between judgments of preference and perception typical of most formal multiattribute decision-making models is questioned in favor of an information-processing formulation in which systematic perceptual errors are associated with, and revealing of, underlying preferences. A model and methodology is proposed for measuring the preference-perception interaction and hypotheses about such interdependencies are tested in a laboratory experiment.

Green, Paul E.

Bayesian Decision Theory in Pricing Strategy

Journal of Marketing 27 (1) (January 1963), 5–14.

Co-winner of the 1963 Alpha Kappa Psi Award (as of 1996, the Marketing Science Institute H. Paul Root Award)

This article shows how Bayesian statistics, a new and powerful tool for systematically working with management judgments, can be used in the area of pricing analysis.

Green, Paul E.

Hybrid Models for Conjoint Analysis: An Expository Review

Journal of Marketing Research 21 (2) (May 1984), 155–69.

1989 William F. O'Dell Award Winner

Over the past few years hybrid models for conjoint analysis have been developed to reduce data collection effort and time. Hybrid models combine features of self-explicated utility measurement with more traditional conjoint analysis. A classification of hybrid models is presented, followed by a review of their comparative performance in cross-validation tests. Though hybrid models represent an attempt to cope with an important practical problem in industry applications of conjoint techniques, these models entail a number of untested assumptions requiring further theoretical analysis and empirical research. Suggestions are offered on future studies that are essential before the role of hybrid models in conjoint methods can be evaluated properly.

Green, Paul E., J. Douglas Carroll, and Stephen M. Goldberg
A General Approach to Product Design Optimization Via Conjoint Analysis
Journal of Marketing 45 (3) (Summer 1981), 17–37.
Co-winner of the 1981 Alpha Kappa Psi Award (as of 1996, the Marketing Science Institute H. Paul Root Award)

This paper describes some of the features of POSSE (Product Optimization and Selected Segment Evaluation), a general procedure for optimizing product/service designs in marketing research. The approach uses input data based on conjoint analysis methods. The output of consumer choice simulators is modeled by means of response surface techniques and optimized by different sets of procedures, depending upon the nature of the objective function.

Green, Paul E., and Abba M. Krieger
Segmenting Markets with Conjoint Analysis
Journal of Marketing 55 (4) (October 1991), 20–31.
1991 Alpha Kappa Psi Award Winner (as of 1996, the Marketing Science Institute H. Paul Root Award)
An earlier version of this paper appeared as MSI Report No. 91–106, "Modeling Competitive Pricing and Market Share: Anatomy of a Decision Support System."

Conjoint analysis is a useful measurement method for implementing market segmentation and product positioning. The authors describe how recently developed optimal product design models provide a way to test the effectiveness of a selected class of market targeting strategies. They first propose a conceptual framework for describing segmentation in the context of conjoint analysis input data. Then they apply that framework to an illustrative case study entailing physicians' preferences for a newly developed prescription drug. They conclude with a discussion of the limitations of the proposed method.

Grover, Rajiv, and V. Srinivasan
A Simultaneous Approach to Market Segmentation and Market Structuring
Journal of Marketing Research 24 (2) (May 1987), 139–53.
1992 William F. O'Dell Award Winner

The authors define a market segment to be a group of consumers homogeneous in terms of the probabilities of choosing the different brands in a product class. Because the vector of choice probabilities is homogeneous within segments and heterogeneous across segments, each segment is characterized by its corresponding group of brands with "large" choice probabilities. The competitive market structure is determined as the possibly overlapping groups of brands corresponding to the different segments. The use of brand choice probabilities as the basis for segmentation leads to market structuring and market segmentation becoming reverse sides of the same analysis. Using panel data, the authors obtain the matrix of cross-classification of brands chosen on two purchase occasions and extract segments by using the maximum likelihood method for estimating latent class models. An application to the instant coffee market indicates that the proposed approach has substantial validity and suggests the presence of submarkets related to product attributes as well as to brand names.

Hauser, John R., and Kenneth J. Wisniewski

Application, Predictive Test, and Strategy Implications for a Dynamic Model of Consumer Response

Marketing Science 1 (2) (Spring 1982), 143–79.
1982 Best Paper Award Winner (as of 1988, the John D.C. Little Award)

This paper describes and evaluates the application of a dynamic stochastic model of consumer response. The model describes, then forecasts, how consumers respond to a new transportation service and to the marketing strategies used during its introduction. The model is estimated on survey data during the first 11 weeks of service. Forecasts over the next 19 weeks are then compared to actual ridership as measured by dispatch records. The model is simple. At any point in time, consumers are described by a set of "behavioral states," indicating (1) whether they are aware of the new service (DART) and (2) what mode of transportation was used for their last trip. Behavior is described by movement among behavioral states; e.g., if a car user tries DART, he makes a transition from "car used for last trip" to "DART used for last trip." The transition probabilities and the rate of transition are dependent on marketing strategies (direct mail, publicity), word of mouth, consumer perceptions, availability of a mode, and budget allocation to transportation. The advantages and disadvantages of the model and the measurements are discussed with respect to predictive ability and managerial utility.

Hoffman, Donna L., and George R. Franke

Correspondence Analysis: Graphical Representation of Categorical Data in Marketing Research

Journal of Marketing Research 23 (3) (August 1986), 213–27.

1991 William F. O'Dell Award Winner

Correspondence analysis is an exploratory data analysis technique for the graphical display of contingency tables and multivariate categorical data. Its history can be traced back at least 50 years under a variety of names, but it has received little attention in the marketing literature. Correspondence analysis scales the rows and columns of a rectangular data matrix in corresponding units so that each can be displayed graphically in the same low-dimensional space. The authors present the theory behind the method, illustrate its use and interpretation with an example representing soft drink consumption, and discuss its relationship to other approaches that jointly represent the rows and columns of a rectangular data matrix.

Jain, Dipak C., and Naufel J. Vilcassim

Investigating Household Purchase Timing Decisions: A Conditional Hazard Function Approach

Marketing Science 10 (1) (Winter 1991), 1–23.

1991 John D. C. Little Award Winner

The purchase timing decision is an important component of the dynamics of a household's purchase behavior. This decision is influenced by marketing and other variables, and the modeling of this dependence has recently received attention in the literature. In this paper, we build on previous studies and develop a comprehensive stochastic model that incorporates the major factors influencing interpurchase times. Specifically, we use a generalized version of Cox's proportional hazard model to test among competing probability distributions for the interpurchase times while incorporating effects due to marketing variables, observed household characteristics, and unobserved heterogeneity across households. The empirical finding from analyzing the IRI coffee data suggests that the interpurchase times cannot be adequately described by probability distributions such as exponential, Erlang-2 or Weibull. The effects of unobserved heterogeneity are significant, and they impact the estimates of the effects of the covariates. We also find that a nonparametric procedure for estimating the effects of unobserved heterogeneity provides the best overall fit to the data and yields covariate estimates that are more consistent with prior expectations. Our model is validated by replicating the substantive empirical findings on an additional product category.

Johnson, Richard M.

Trade-off Analysis of Consumer Values

Journal of Marketing Research 11 (2) (May 1974), 121–7.

Co-winner of the 1979 William F. O'Dell Award

A method for exploring and quantifying the value systems of consumers through conjoint measurement is described. Since it is concerned with value systems of individual consumers, the method is most appropriate for product categories where consumers' desires are heterogeneous and where markets are highly segmented.

Levy, Sidney J.

Interpreting Consumer Mythology: A Structural Approach to Consumer Behavior

Journal of Marketing 45 (3) (Summer 1981), 49–61.

1981 Harold H. Maynard Award Winner

Consumer behavior depth interviews are grouped with other kinds of story telling—fairy tales, novels, psychological test responses, and myths—as imaginative statements that can be qualitatively interpreted for their functional and symbolic content. Drawing upon the Claude Levi-Strauss approach to the analysis of myths, a structuralist interpretation illustrates application to the age, sex, and social status dimensions of food consumption.

Little, John D. C.

Decision Support Systems for Marketing Managers

Journal of Marketing 43 (3) (Summer 1979), 9–26.

1979 Alpha Kappa Psi Award Winner (as of 1996, the Marketing Science Institute H. Paul Root Award)

In the past 10 years, a new technology has emerged for assisting and improving marketing decision making. We define a marketing decision support system as a coordinated collection of data, models, analytic tools, and computing power by which an organization gathers information from the environment and turns it into a basis for action. Where such systems have taken root, they have grown and become increasingly productive for their organizations.

Lynch, John G., Jr.

Uniqueness Issues in the Decompositional Modeling of Multiattribute Overall Evaluations: An Information Integration Perspective

Journal of Marketing Research 22 (1) (February 1985), 1–19.

1990 William F. O'Dell Award Winner

The author reviews how methods developed within the information integration paradigm can be used to study consumers' overall evaluations of choice alternatives. Methods are presented for determining the adequacy of several common model forms used to represent overall evaluations: adding, multiplying, and multilinear. Often, more than one integration model can be reconciled with the data by altering one's assumptions about the subjective values of the independent variables and about the relationship between private, unobservable overall evaluations and the overt numerical ratings that index them. Also, different integration models lead to parameter estimates (e.g., part worths) of varying levels of uniqueness and interattribute comparability.

Emphasis is given to pinpointing the sorts of evidence and experimental designs that enable one to distinguish empirically among alternative model forms and psychological interpretations of the data—and, conversely, to what interpretations cannot be distinguished empirically—given only overall evaluations of a set of choice alternatives that vary along two or more attribute dimensions. Finally, the methods described are compared with model diagnosis procedures more commonly used in marketing and consumer research, including compositional correlational techniques and decompositional methods of conjoint measurement.

Mick, David Glen

Consumer Research and Semiotics: Exploring the Morphology of Signs, Symbols, and Significance

Journal of Consumer Research 13 (2) (September 1986), 196–213.

1989 Association for Consumer Research Best Article Award Winner (as of 1996, the *Journal of Consumer Research* Best Article Award)

The importance of signs and symbols has been widely recognized, but only a handful of consumer researchers have developed theory and research programs based on semiotics, the doctrine of signs. This article outlines the emergence and principal perspectives of semiotics and then discusses its applications and implications for consumer research. Among its strengths, semiotics positions meaning at the nucleus of consumer behavior, provides a rich metalanguage for semiotic consumer research, and recommends a multi-paradigm philosophy of science.

Perreault, William D., Jr., and Forrest W. Young

Alternating Least Squares Optimal Scaling: Analysis of Nonmetric Data in Marketing Research

Journal of Marketing Research 17 (1) (February 1980), 1–13.

1985 William F. O'Dell Award Winner

The authors discuss and illustrate the advantages and limitations of a family of new approaches to the analysis of metric and nonmetric data in marketing research. The general method, which is based on alternating least squares optimal scaling procedures, extends the analytical flexibility of the general linear model procedures (ANOVA, regression, canonical correlation, discriminant analysis, etc.) to situations in which the data (1) are measured at any mixture of the nominal, ordinal, or interval levels and (2) are derived from either a discrete or continuous distribution. The relationship of these procedures to traditional linear models and to other nonmetric approaches (such as multidimensional scaling and conjoint analysis) is reviewed.

Peter, J. Paul

Construct Validity: A Review of Basic Issues and Marketing Practices

Journal of Marketing Research 18 (2) (May 1981), 133–45.

1986 William F. O'Dell Award Winner

An attempt is made to explicate the meaning of construct validity. Operational issues in the process of construct validation are investigated. A subset of JMR studies involving construct validation are reviewed and the role of construct validity in marketing is considered.

Roberts, Harry V.

Bayesian Statistics in Marketing

Journal of Marketing 27 (1) (January 1963), 1–4.

Co-winner of the 1963 Alpha Kappa Psi Award (as of 1996, the Marketing Science Institute H. Paul Root Award)

Bayesian statistics points the way to an articulation of business judgment and statistical research in approaching marketing problems. We have always known that neither executive nor statistician is sufficient in himself, but now for the first time we have formal tools that show that the two can be brought closer together. This article shows how this may be accomplished.

Srivastava, Rajendra K., Mark I. Alpert, and Allan D. Shocker

A Customer-Oriented Approach for Determining Market Structures

Journal of Marketing 48 (2) (Spring 1984), 32–45.

1984 Alpha Kappa Psi Award Winner (as of 1996, the Marketing Science Institute H. Paul Root Award)

A framework for market analysis based on customer perceptions of substitutability-in-use is presented. An empirical application in the financial/banking services market is used to illustrate that when product preferences are dependent on the use/consumption context (especially relevant when products have multiple uses), situational variables can help predictive ability, and hierarchical clusters (requiring exclusive group membership) may be misleading. Additionally, it is shown that interactions among situation, product, and person factors may be more managerially meaningful than the main effects.

Ter Hofstede, Frenkel, Jan-Benedict E. M. Steenkamp, and Michel Wedel

International Market Segmentation Based on Consumer-Product Relations

Journal of Marketing Research 36 (1) (February 1999), 1–17.

2004 William F. O'Dell Award Winner

With increasing competition in the global marketplace, international segmentation has become an ever more important issue in developing, positioning, and selling products across national borders. The authors propose a methodology to identify cross-national market segments, based on means-end chain theory. The methodology offers the potential for integrating product development and communication strategies by linking product characteristics to consumer benefits and values. For that purpose, a model is developed that identifies relations between the consumer and the product at the segment level, which increases the actionability and responsiveness of the segments. The model accounts for different response tendencies, across and within countries, that commonly hamper identification of cross-national segments. A Monte Carlo study shows that the model performs well in recovering the parameters across a wide range of conditions. The segmentation model is applied to consumer data on yogurt collected in 11 countries of the European Union. Four international segments are identified and found to be related to consumer sociodemographics, consumption patterns, media consumption, and personality. The authors show that the model has high predictive validity and outperforms the standard clustering approaches traditionally employed in international segmentation.

Toubia, Olivier, Duncan I. Simester, John R. Hauser, and Ely Dahan

Fast Polyhedral Adaptive Conjoint Estimation

Marketing Science 22 (3) (Summer 2003), 273–303.
Co-winner of the 2003 John D. C. Little Award and the 2004 Frank M. Bass Dissertation Paper
Award

We propose and test new adaptive question design and estimation algorithms for partial profile conjoint analysis. Polyhedral question design focuses questions to reduce a feasible set of parameters as rapidly as possible. Analytic center estimation uses a centrality criterion based on consistency with respondents' answers. Both algorithms run with no noticeable delay between questions.

We evaluate the proposed methods relative to established benchmarks for question design (random selection, D-efficient designs, adaptive conjoint analysis) and estimation (hierarchical Bayes). Monte Carlo simulations vary respondent heterogeneity and response errors. For low numbers of questions, polyhedral question design does best (or is tied for best) for all tested domains. For high numbers of questions, efficient fixed designs do better in some domains. Analytic center estimation shows promise for high heterogeneity and for low response errors; hierarchical Bayes for low heterogeneity and high response errors. Other simulations evaluate hybrid methods, which include self-explicated data.

A field test (330 respondents) compared methods on both internal validity (holdout tasks) and external validity (actual choice of a laptop bag worth approximately $100). The field test is consistent with the simulation results and offers strong support for polyhedral question design. In addition, marketplace sales were consistent with conjoint-analysis predictions.

Wells, William D.

Psychographics: A Critical Review

Journal of Marketing Research 12 (2) (May 1975), 196–213.
1980 William F. O'Dell Award Winner

This article presents case histories of five somewhat different uses of psychographic research, and it critically reviews the status of research in this field.

Wind, Yoram

A New Procedure for Concept Evaluation

Journal of Marketing 37 (4) (October 1973), 2–11.

1973 Alpha Kappa Psi Award Winner (as of 1996, the Marketing Science Institute H. Paul Root Award)

The author suggests a concept testing procedure which relies on concept evaluation and positioning by market segments. The integration of multidimensional scaling, conjoint measurement procedures, and related multivariate statistical techniques is explained and illustrated.

Additional Relevant Papers: Research Tools

Ansari, Asim, and Carl F. Mela

E-Customization

Journal of Marketing Research 40 (2) (May 2003), 131–45. See page 54 for abstract.

Co-winner of the 2004 Paul E. Green Award

Arndt, Johan

On Making Marketing Science More Scientific: Role of Orientations, Paradigms, Metaphors, and Puzzle Solving

Journal of Marketing 49 (3) (Summer 1985), 11–23. See page 68 for abstract.

1985 Harold H. Maynard Award Winner

Brucks, Merrie

The Effects of Product Class Knowledge on Information Search Behavior

Journal of Consumer Research 12 (1) (June 1985), 1–16. See page 150 for abstract.

1984 Robert Ferber Award Winner

Bult, Jan Roelf, and Tom Wansbeek

Optimal Selection for Direct Mail

Marketing Science 14 (4) (Autumn 1995), 378–94. See page 55 for abstract.

1995 Frank M. Bass Dissertation Paper Award Winner

Dekimpe, Marnik G., and Dominique M. Hanssens

Sustained Spending and Persistent Response: A New Look at Long-Term Marketing Profitability

Journal of Marketing Research 36 (4) (November 1999), 397–412. See page 40 for abstract.

2000 Paul E. Green Award Winner

Dillon, William R., Thomas J. Madden, Amna Kirmani, and Soumen Mukherjee
Understanding What's in a Brand Rating: A Model for Assessing Brand and Attribute Effects and Their Relationship to Brand Equity
Journal of Marketing Research 38 (4) (November 2001), 415–29. See page 28 for abstract.
2002 Paul E. Green Award Winner

Griffin, Abbie, and John R. Hauser
The Voice of the Customer
Marketing Science 12 (1) (Winter 1993), 1–27. See page 16 for abstract.
1993 John D. C. Little Award Winner and 1994 Frank M. Bass Dissertation Paper Award Winner

Gupta, Sunil
Impact of Sales Promotions on When, What, and How Much to Buy
Journal of Marketing Research 25 (4) (November 1988), 342–55. See page 121 for abstract.
1993 William F. O'Dell Award Winner

Krishnamurthi, Lakshman, and S. P. Raj
A Model of Brand Choice and Purchase Quantity Price Sensitivities
Marketing Science 7 (1) (Winter 1988), 1–20. See page 123 for abstract.
Co-winner of the 1988 John D. C. Little Award

Richins, Marsha L.
Measuring Emotions in the Consumption Experience
Journal of Consumer Research 24 (2) (September 1997), 127–46. See page 157 for abstract.
Co-winner of the 2000 *Journal of Consumer Research* Best Article Award

Rindfleisch, Aric, and Jan B. Heide
Transaction Cost Analysis: Past, Present, and Future Applications
Journal of Marketing 61 (4) (October 1997), 30–54. See page 58 for abstract.
1997 Harold H. Maynard Award Winner and 2004 Louis W. Stern Award Winner

Roberts, John H., and James M. Lattin
Development and Testing of a Model of Consideration Set Composition
Journal of Marketing Research 28 (4) (November 1991), 429–40. See page 131 for abstract.
1996 William F. O'Dell Award Winner

Shocker, Allan D., and V. Srinivasan

Multiattribute Approaches for Product Concept Evaluation and Generation: A Critical Review

Journal of Marketing Research 16 (2) (May 1979), 159–80. See page 20 for abstract.

1984 William F. O'Dell Award Winner

Silk, Alvin J., and Glen L. Urban

Pre-Test-Market Evaluation of New Packaged Goods: A Model and Measurement Methodology

Journal of Marketing Research 15 (2) (May 1978), 171–91. See page 20 for abstract.

1983 William F. O'Dell Award Winner

Urban, Glen L., and Gerald M. Katz

Pre-Test-Market Models: Validation and Managerial Implications

Journal of Marketing Research 20 (3) (August 1983), 221–34. See page 21 for abstract.

1988 William F. O'Dell Award Winner

Urban, Glen L., Bruce D. Weinberg, and John R. Hauser

Premarket Forecasting of Really-New Products

Journal of Marketing 60 (1) (January 1996), 47–60. See page 21 for abstract.

1996 Marketing Science Institute/H. Paul Root Award Winner

van Heerde, Harald J., Sachin Gupta, and Dick R. Wittink

Is 75% of the Sales Promotion Bump Due to Brand Switching? No, Only 33% Is

Journal of Marketing Research 40 (4) (November 2003), 481–91. See page 134 for abstract.

Co-winner of the 2004 Paul E. Green Award

7

Marketing Mix

In this chapter, we cover prize-winning papers that deal with the elements of the marketing mix: product, price, place, and promotion. In the section on product, we cover only those papers related to product management, since papers on the development of new products are covered in Chapter 1, "New Products, Growth, and Innovation." The section on price contains both papers focused on a brand's regular price and papers that consider the marketplace reaction to promotional price cuts. Since manufacturer-retailer interactions are covered in the chapter on customer management, we cover prize-winning papers related to important retailer decisions in the section on place. In the promotion section, we cover prize-winning papers that deal with advertising.

Product

These papers cover consumers' decisions to consider and buy new products, manufacturers' problems in positioning and extending products, and product or service quality and profitability.

Consideration and Purchase

In launching a new product, an early goal is to get consumers to consider the new product. Roberts and Lattin (1991) offered a model of consideration set formation in which a new product's likelihood of entering a consumer's consideration set is based on the tradeoff between the utility the consumer expects from the product and effort required to add that product to the consumer's extant consideration set. Once considered, the product must be purchased. Heilman, Bowman, and Wright (2000) began their framework with a consumer's first-ever purchase in a product category and described the evolution of purchase behavior, assuming that consumers want to learn about options but are also risk averse.

Positioning and Extending an Existing Product

Conventional product strategy, going back as far as Politz (1960) and Wind and Claycamp (1976), suggests that one should distinguish a product from competitors on an attribute that is relevant, meaningful, and valuable to consumers. Carpenter, Glazer, and Nakamoto (1994) showed that a product can be successfully differentiated on an irrelevant attribute if consumers believe that the attribute might be relevant under certain conditions. Ofek and Srinivasan (2002) provided a measure of the market value of any potential product modification. Comparing that value to the incremental unit cost of the modification allows the manufacturer to determine whether that attribute improvement would be profitable.

Product or Service Quality and Profitability

Using PIMS data, Jacobson and Aaker (1987) showed that higher levels of product or service quality are associated with higher levels of profitability. With this understanding of the importance of service quality, Zeithaml (1988) touched off a service quality research stream by focusing on quality as perceived by consumers when many companies were still defining and measuring quality from the company's perspective. Prize-winning papers related to service quality can be found in Chapter 4, "Managing Relationships with Customers and Organizations."

Price

In this section we cover papers that take the consumer's, the supplier's, and the regulator's perspective on a product or service's regular price. In addition, we consider papers that deal with marketplace reaction to a brand's promotions.

Regular Price

As unit pricing began to be used in supermarkets, Zeithaml (1982) investigated consumers' use of that new pricing information. She found that people who had access to unit price information felt more certain about their recall of relative prices and believed they made decisions that were more economical. However, they did not, in fact, demonstrate better recall of relative prices. She conjectured that they may have read and used the relative price information without assimilating it into memory.

Narasimhan (1984) showed that coupons—price discrimination devices—are used by consumers who are more price elastic and have higher opportunity cost of time. Taking the suppliers' perspective, Bakos and Brynjolfsson (1999) found that suppliers achieve higher sales and higher profit per good if they bundle a large number of information goods and sell that bundle at a fixed price. This happens because it is easier to predict consumers' valuations of a bundle of goods than it is to predict their valuation of the individual goods. Desiraju and Shugan (1999) investigated the profitability of different pricing strategies for capacity-constrained services using techniques from yield management systems. They showed that early discounting, overbooking, and limiting early sales only improve profits for services when price-insensitive customers arrive late (i.e., have high commitment costs). They showed that yield management systems usually will not work when arrivals fail to follow this pattern. Xie and Shugan (2001) examined situations in which purchase occurs before the time of consumption. They found that in such situations, unlike with yield management, which is driven by price discrimination, the profit advantage of advance selling is not limited to capacity-constrained businesses with late-arriving customers who are less price sensitive than early-arriving customers. Instead, the relative profit advantage from advance selling is driven by consumer uncertainty about future consumption states. They also showed that binding capacity constraints create two very different effects: the constraints raise spot prices and sometimes raise advance prices above spot prices.

Sudhir (2001) showed with structural analysis and scanner data that when one assumes that retailers set prices to maximize category profit rather than to hold margin constant, the inferred level of manufacturer pricing is less cooperative, consistent with Bertrand competition.

Marketplace Reactions to a Brand's Promotions

As early as 1965, Barton (1965) proposed a model of market response that recognized the importance of distinguishing between sales made at a brand's regular price and sales made when the brand is on promotion. Blattberg and Wisniewski (1989) showed that the pattern of promotion sales differs across brands. Higher-price, higher-quality brands, when promoted, take share from all brands in the market, but lower-price, lower-quality brands, when promoted, only take share from other lower-price, lower-quality brands.

Krishnamurthi and Raj (1988) included both the brand choice decision and the quantity decision in a single model and showed that consumers consider prices of all of the competitive brands in the brand choice decision but consider only the price of the chosen brand in the quantity decision. Gupta (1988) included the brand choice, the quantity decision, and the purchase incidence decision in his model. His decomposition of promotion elasticities showed that 84% of promotional sales increase is due to brand switching, 14% is due to purchase acceleration, and 2% is due to stockpiling. Van Heerde, Gupta, and Wittink (2003) showed that a transformation of the decomposition of promotion elasticities into a unit sales decomposition indicates that on average only 33% of the sales increase due to a temporary price cut comes from brand switching.

Raju, Srinivasan, and Lal (1990) considered the impact of brand loyalty on promotion effectiveness and showed that weaker brands gain more from price promotion than do stronger brands. Assunção and Meyer (1993) showed how promotions can cause increased consumption (thereby increasing category demand). According to their model, when consumers hold more inventory, they should rationally increase consumption; inventories should be largest when promotions occur at intermediate frequencies (though below 50%). The mechanism that drives this is consumer uncertainty about the future prices of goods. Variably timed price promotions encourage stockpiling, which, in turn, should encourage increased consumption by decreasing the expected future price of the good.

Kivetz (2005) considered the impact of reactance on promotion effectiveness and showed that offering promotional rewards that are consistent with the promoted consumption effort allows consumers to construe their behavior as intrinsically motivated rather than externally induced, thereby muting reactance.

Place

In this section, we focus on two important decisions that a retailer must make: how to arrange products on shelves and how to set prices. Bultez and Naert (1988) generalized existing models for shelf-space allocation by incorporating demand interdependencies across and within product categories. Broniarczyk, Hoyer, and McAlister (1998) studied the amount of variety consumers perceive when they view a retailer's shelf set. In lab tests and a field study, they showed that if total shelf space for a category is held constant and if the favorite brand is available, the number of different products offered in the category can be substantially reduced without affecting perceptions of the amount of variety offered.

Two additional papers considered the implications of a retailer's decision to use a Hi-Lo pricing strategy or an EDLP (everyday low price) strategy. In two field experiments, Hoch, Drèze, and Purk (1994), studying individual categories in isolation, found that a 10% price change in an EDLP category resulted in only a 3% volume change; they concluded that, given that low level of responsiveness, a Hi-Lo strategy was more profitable for a category than an EDLP strategy. Bell and Lattin (1998) considered the impact of store price format on store choice. They found that EDLP stores got a greater-than-expected share of business from large-basket shoppers, while Hi-Lo stores got a greater-than-expected share from small-basket shoppers, potentially reversing Hoch, Drèze, and Purk's finding that Hi-Lo is more profitable than EDLP.

Promotion

One of the early winners of research awards, Coffin (1963) reported that advertising effectiveness has two dimensions: size of audience and depth of impact. He encouraged work on depth of impact, which had not received as much attention as size of audience. Maloney (1963) gave structure to that call by pointing out that an ad's depth of impact depends on the interaction of the ad with consumers' attitudes. When the FTC became concerned about the potential for deceptive advertising, Gardner (1975) built on the notion that ads interact with consumers' attitudes to propose a plan for detecting deceptive advertising. In a similar vein, Pechmann and Knight (2002) showed that after being exposed to cigarette advertising, ninth graders had favorable thoughts about unfamiliar peers who smoked, whereas ninth graders exposed to antismoking ads in conjunction with cigarette advertising had unfavorable thoughts about unfamiliar peers who smoked.

Repetition and Liking

In an effort to understand how ads might affect attitudes, researchers looked at psychological evidence that suggested that "mere exposure" to advertising could increase liking for the product advertised, and that repeated exposure could increasing liking even more. Obermiller (1985) showed that there was no support for the notion that liking occurs without cognitive mediation. Building on that theme, Burke and Srull (1988) showed that repetition had a positive effect on recall of the advertisement only if there was, essentially, no advertising for other, similar products.

Wearout and Pulsed Advertisements

Naik, Mantrala, and Sawyer (1998) showed that pulsed advertising can generate greater total awareness than can continuous advertising if wearout occurs. Nordhielm (2002) showed that wearout occurs for features of the ad that are processed deeply but not for features of the ad that are processed shallowly.

The Influence of Ads on Interpretation of Product Use

Moore and Lutz (2000) showed that for 7- to 8-year-old children, advertisements don't frame product trials, but for 10- to 11-year-olds, advertisements can shape the interpretation of subsequent usage experience. Although younger children have traditionally been viewed as most vulnerable to advertising, this set of studies suggests that while older children have the cognitive capacity to process an ad and trial experience in a relatively complex fashion, they may not spontaneously invoke their cognitive defenses when needed. Braun (1999), studying adults, showed that advertisements can change what subjects learn from product experience. When questioned after product use, people indicate that their product experience has been as suggested by the advertising.

Short-term Impact on Sales

Lodish et al.'s (1995) meta-analysis of 389 real-world advertising experiments found that ads are more effective for new products, consistent with Maloney (1963) and perhaps at least partially explained by Moore and Lutz (2000) and Braun (1999). Lodish et al. also found that changes in brand, copy, and media strategy enhance advertising effectiveness, consistent with the pulsing results in Naik, Mantrala, and Sawyer (1998) and Nordhielm (2002).

Long-term Impact on Sales

Clarke (1976) looked across studies of the long-run impact of advertising and showed that the interval between observations influences the estimated duration of the advertising effect. He concluded that the cumulative advertising effect lasts not years, but months. Givon and Horsky (1990) went further and suggested that the long-term effects attributed to cumulative advertising may instead be the result of purchase reinforcement.

Market Power versus Information

Mitra and Lynch (1995) reconciled competing economic theories of advertising: one theory held that advertising creates market power, thereby lowering price elasticity; the other held that advertising provides information, thereby increasing price elasticity. Mitra and Lynch observed that when point-of-purchase information is either too scarce or too overwhelming, consumers' consideration sets are influenced by advertising recall. Higher levels of advertising drive higher levels of recall, expanding consumers' consideration sets, and thereby increasing price elasticity. When recall isn't an important influence in the formation of consumers' consideration sets (i.e., when there is an appropriate amount of information at point of purchase), there is no recall effect, and differentiation advertising gives brands market power, lowering price elasticity.

Consumer/Culture Adaptation

In an early prize-winning paper, White (1959) pointed out the importance, when trying to understand the potential impact of brand advertising, of considering the cultural meaning of the brand. More recently, prize-winning papers have considered a causal link between brand advertising and culture. O'Guinn and Shrum (1997) showed that exposure to consumption-rich television portrayals systematically increases consumers' estimates of the real-world prevalence of goods and services: the more television one watches, the more hot tubs, sports cars, and other trappings of affluence one believes there are. For their part, Ritson and Elliott (1999) showed the impact of advertising on culture; their study showed how advertising copy is integrated into the language and lives of British adolescents. Consistent with this theme of adaptation in response to marketing actions, Friestad and Wright (1994) tell us that "the effects of [marketing/persuasion] tactics may be altered by people's gaining awareness of them, incorporating beliefs about them in their persuasion knowledge, and using that knowledge when processing a persuasion attempt. [The effects of marketing/persuasion tactics] may continue to be altered as long as people's interpretations and evaluations of the tactics, and their strategies for coping with them, keep changing" (p. 24).

Research Priorities

MSI corporate members want to know how such elements of the marketing mix as advertisements, customer experiences, nonverbal brand elements, corporate logos, and so forth impact sales, price premium, sales call effectiveness, distribution, employee motivation, brand equity, and firm value. They want to understand how that impact changes across cultures and geographies and as media become more fragmented. They are interested in incorporating nontraditional media (e.g., product placements, sponsorships, "buzz marketing") and in-store marketing (special packaging, in-store media, shelving) in marketing mix models. They want tools to help coordinate all customer communications and to allocate budgets across elements of the marketing mix, media, markets, geographic regions, etc. They want to know how to price optimally over time and over the product life cycle, and how to anticipate and influence competitors' pricing. They want to understand the organizational issues involved in making pricing decisions and in formulating and implementing pricing strategies.

Abstracts: Marketing Mix

Assunção, João L., and Robert J. Meyer

The Rational Effect of Price Promotions on Sales and Consumption

Management Science 39 (50 (May 1993), 517–35.
1993 Frank M. Bass Dissertation Paper Award Winner

We explore the rational effect of price variation on sales and consumption in markets where consumers are uncertain about the future price of goods. We first derive an optimal ordering policy which expresses the amount a consumer should purchase and consume in a given period as a function of the observed price of the good, the distribution of future prices, and the nature of his or her inventory. This policy extends previous normative models of inventory control, such as those by Golabi (1985) and Kalymon (1970) to the case where the amount to consume in a given period is an explicit decision variable and prices follow a first-order stochastic process. We then use this model to explore how changes in the long-run frequency and temporal correlations of price promotions should normatively affect the contemporaneous relationship between purchase, consumption and price. Among the predictions which follow from the model are that consumption should rationally increase with the size of existing inventories, the short-term sensitivity of sales to prices should be greater than that of consumption to price, and this discrepancy increases with decreases in the temporal correlation of price deals and the long-term relative frequency of price deals.

Bakos, Yannis, and Erik Brynjolfsson

Bundling Information Goods: Pricing, Profits, and Efficiency

Management Science 45 (12) (December 1999), 1613–30.
1999 John D. C. Little Award Winner

We study the strategy of bundling a large number of information goods, such as those increasingly available on the Internet, and selling them for a fixed price. We analyze the optimal bundling strategies for a multiproduct monopolist, and we find that bundling very large numbers of unrelated information goods can be surprisingly profitable. The reason is that the law of large numbers makes it much easier to predict consumers' valuations for a bundle of goods than their valuations for the individual goods when sold separately. As a result, this "predictive value of bundling" makes it possible to achieve greater sales, greater economic efficiency, and greater profits per good from a bundle of information goods than can be attained when the same goods are sold separately. Our main results do not extend to most physical goods, as the marginal costs of production for goods not used by the buyer typically negate any benefits from the predictive value of large-scale bundling. While determining optimal bundling strategies for more than two goods is a notoriously difficult problem, we use statistical techniques to provide strong asymptotic results and bounds on profits for bundles of any arbitrary size. We show how our model can be used to analyze the bundling of complements and substitutes, bundling in the presence of budget constraints, and bundling of goods with various types of correlations and how each of these conditions can lead to limits on optimal bundle size. In particular we find that when different market segments of consumers differ systematically in their valuations for goods, simple bundling will no longer be optimal. However, by offering a menu of different bundles aimed at each market segment, bundling makes traditional price discrimination strategies more powerful by reducing the role of unpredictable idiosyncratic components of valuations. The predictions of our analysis appear to be consistent with empirical observations of the markets for Internet and online content, cable television programming, and copyrighted music.

Barton, Samuel G.
A Marketing Model for Short-Term Prediction of Consumer Sales
Journal of Marketing 29 (3) (July 1965), 19–29.
1965 Alpha Kappa Psi Award Winner (as of 1996, the Marketing Science Institute H. Paul Root Award)

This article is a nontechnical description of a generalized marketing model from the point of view of the manufacturer of nondurable goods, one who does not fully control his own distribution system. The model seeks to identify the main marketing variables affecting the sales of such products. These are arranged in a structure which offers a useful conceptual approach for marketing management, and a starting framework for a specific information-system design. Mr. Barton believes that it is technically feasible to collect input statistics with sufficient accuracy as to improve the marketing activities of many medium-size to large-size companies.

Bell, David R., and James M. Lattin

Shopping Behavior and Consumer Preference for Store Price Format: Why "Large Basket" Shoppers Prefer EDLP

Marketing Science 17 (1) (Winter 1998), 66–88.

1999 Frank M. Bass Dissertation Paper Award Winner

An earlier version of this paper appeared as MSI Report No. 98–114.

In recent years, the supermarket industry has become increasingly competitive. One outcome has been the proliferation of a variety of pricing formats, and considerable debate among academics and practitioners about how these formats affect consumers' store choice behavior. This paper advances the idea that consumer shopping behavior (as defined by average size of the shopping basket and the frequency of store visits) is an important determinant of the store choice decision when stores offer different price formats. A recent *Wall Street Journal* article that summarized the result of Bruno's management switching the chain from EDLP to HILO illustrates the important of this issue: "The company's price-conscious customers, used to shopping for a fixed basket of goods, stayed away in droves." Thus, the audience for this paper includes practitioners and academics who wish to understand store choices or predict how a change in price format might affect store profitability and the mix of clientele that shop there.

This paper attempts to understand the relationship between grocery shopping behavior, retail price format, and store choice by posing and answering the following questions. First, after controlling for other factors (e.g., distance to the store, prior experience in the store, advertised specials), do consumer expectations about prices for a basket of grocery products ("expected basket attractiveness") influence the store choice decision? This is a fairly straightforward test of the effect of price expectations on store choice. Second, are different pricing formats (EDLP or HILO) more or less attractive to different types of shoppers? To adequately answer the second question, we must link consumers' category purchase decisions, which collectively define the market basket, and the store choice decision.

We study the research questions using two complementary approaches. First, we develop a stylized theory of consumer shopping behavior under price uncertainty. The principal features and results from the stylized model can be summarized as follows. Shoppers are defined (in a relative sense) as either large or small basket shoppers. Thus, we abstract from the vicissitudes of individual shopping trips and focus on meaningful differences across shoppers in terms of the expected basket size per trip. The shoppers make category purchase incidence decisions and can choose to shop in either an EDLP or a HILO store. Large basket shoppers are shoppers who have a relatively high probability of purchase for any given category, and as such they are more captive to prices across many different categories. The first two propositions summarize the price responsiveness of shoppers. In particular, the large basket shoppers are less responsive to price in their individual category purchase incidence decisions; this makes them more responsive to the expected basket price in their store choice decisions. This key structural implication of the model highlights an asymmetry between response at the category level and response at the store level.

The result is quite intuitive; a (large basket) shopper with less ability to respond to prices in individual product categories will be more sensitive to the expected cost of the overall portfolio (the market basket) when choosing a store. The final proposition derives the price at which a given shopper will be indifferent between an EDLP and a HILO store. The key insight is that as a shopper increases his or her tendency to become a large basket shopper, the EDLP store can increase its (constant) price closer and closer to the average price in the HILO store. Conversely, as the shopper becomes more of small basket shopper, the EDLP store must lower its price closer to the deal price in the HILO store. Thus, we have the interesting result that small basket shoppers prefer HILO stores, even at higher average prices.

The empirical testing mirrors the development of the consumer theory. We test the implications of the propositions using a market basket scanner panel database. The database includes two years of shopping data for 1,042 households in two separate market areas. We first use household-level grocery expenditures to model the probability that a household is a large or small basket shopper. Subsequently, we estimate purchase incidence and store choice models. We find that after controlling for important factors such as household distance to the store, previous experience in the store, and advertised specials, price expectations for the basket influence store choice. Furthermore, EDLP stores get a greater than expected share of business from large basket shoppers; HILO stores get a greater than expected share from small basket shoppers. Consistent with the implications of the propositions, large basket shoppers are relatively price inelastic in their category purchase incidence decisions and price elastic in their store choice decisions.

Blattberg, Robert C., and Kenneth J. Wisniewski
Price-Induced Patterns of Competition
Marketing Science 8 (4) (Autumn 1989), 291–309.
1989 John D. C. Little Award Winner

This research focuses on how price changes influence the observed pattern of brand competition. The paper begins with a basic utility model formulation and examines the implications of three major classes of preference distributions on the expected patterns of competition. A price-tier model is proposed to operationalize the theory and to allow predictive testing. The price-tier model is estimated on 28 brands across four product categories. The results show a specific asymmetric pattern of price competition. Higher-price, higher-quality brands steal share from other brands in the same price-quality tier, as well as from brands in the tier below. However, lower-price, lower-quality brands take sales from their own tier and the tier below brands, but do not steal significant share from the tiers above. The results are consistent with a bimodal preference distribution, with the regular price indifference point being located toward the lower-quality end of the preference distribution for the categories analyzed.

Braun, Kathryn A.

Postexperience Advertising Effects on Consumer Memory

Journal of Consumer Research 25 (4) (March 1999), 319–34.

1999 Robert Ferber Award Winner and 2002 *Journal of Consumer Research* Best Article Award Winner

Past research suggests that marketing communications create expectations that influence the way consumers subsequently learn from their product experiences. Since postexperience information can also be important and is widespread for established goods and services, it is appropriate to ask about the cognitive effects of these efforts. The postexperience advertising situation is conceptualized here as an instant source-forgetting problem where the language and imagery from the recently presented advertising become confused with consumers' own experiential memories. It is suggested that, through a reconstructive memory process, this advertising information affects how and what consumers remember. Consumers may come to believe that their past product experience had been as suggested by the advertising. Over time this postexperience advertising information can become incorporated into the brand schema and influence future product decisions.

Broniarczyk, Susan M., Wayne D. Hoyer, and Leigh McAlister

Consumers' Perceptions of the Assortment Offered in a Grocery Category: The Impact of Item Reduction

Journal of Marketing Research 35 (2) (May 1998), 166–76.

2003 William F. O'Dell Award Winner

An earlier version of this paper appeared as MSI Report No. 97–125.

Grocery retailers have been informed that, to remain competitive, they must reduce the number of stockkeeping units (SKUs) offered, in line with consumer demand, or, in other words, adopt "Efficient Assortment." Retailers have resisted this principle on the basis of a fear that eliminating items would lower consumer assortment perceptions and decrease the likelihood of store choice. In two studies, the authors examine how consumers form assortment perceptions in the face of SKU reduction with a particular emphasis on two heuristic cues: the availability of a favorite product and the amount of shelf space devoted to the category. Results indicate that retailers might be able to make substantive reductions in the number of items carried without negatively affecting assortment perceptions and store choice, as long as only low-preference items are eliminated and category space is held constant. Thus, the potential risk inherent in item reduction might be more limited than initially thought. The authors then discuss the implications of these findings for retailers, as well as additional measurement considerations.

Bultez, Alain, and Philippe Naert
S.H.A.R.P.: Shelf Allocation for Retailers' Profit
Marketing Science 7 (3) (Summer 1988), 211–31.
Co-winner of the 1988 John D. C. Little Award

Shelf space is the retailer's scarcest resource. Space management tools are thus badly needed. For that purpose, commercial computer packages and optimal allocation models have been developed. Building on the work of Corstjens and Doyle, we elaborate a general, theoretical shelf space allocation model, which focuses on the demand interdependencies prevailing across and within product-groups. Rules of thumb are compared to the derived optimal allocation. The SH.A.R.P. model is introduced as a simplified, yet realistic, variant and validated against data collected in a Dutch supermarket chain. Subsequently, the feasibility of its implementation has been [tested] in various Belgian chains. Case studies demonstrate the profit potential of SH.A.R.P.

Burke, Raymond R., and Thomas K. Srull
Competitive Interference and Consumer Memory for Advertising
Journal of Consumer Research 15 (1) (June 1988), 55–68.
1989 Robert Ferber Award Winner

This article reports the results of three experiments that examine memory interference in an advertising context. In Experiment 1, consumer memory for a brand's advertising was inhibited as a result of subsequent exposure to ads for other products in that manufacturer's product line and ads for competing brands in the product class. Experiment 2 demonstrates analogous proactive interference effects. The results of Experiment 3 indicate that the presence of advertising for competitive brands changes the relationship between ad repetition and consumer memory. Repetition had a positive effect on recall only when there was little or no advertising for similar products.

Carpenter, Gregory S., Rashi Glazer, and Kent Nakamoto

Meaningful Brands from Meaningless Differentiation: The Dependence on Irrelevant Attributes

Journal of Marketing Research 31 (3) (August 1994), 339–50.

1999 William F. O'Dell Award Winner

Conventional product differentiation strategies prescribe distinguishing a product or brand from competitors' on the basis of an attribute that is relevant, meaningful, and valuable to consumers. However, brands also successfully differentiate on an attribute that appears to create a meaningful product difference but on closer examination is irrelevant to creating that benefit—"meaningless" differentiation. The authors examine how meaningless differentiation can produce a meaningfully differentiated brand. They argue that buyers may infer that a distinguishing but irrelevant attribute is in fact relevant and valuable under certain conditions, creating a meaningfully differentiated brand. They outline the consumer inference process and develop a set of hypotheses about when it will produce meaningful brands from meaningless differentiation. Experimental tests in three product categories support their analysis. They explore the implications of the results for product differentiation strategies, consumer preference formation, and the nature of competition.

Clarke, Darral G.

Econometric Measurement of the Duration of Advertising Effect on Sales

Journal of Marketing Research 13 (4) (November 1976), 345–57.

Co-winner of the 1981 William F. O'Dell Award

A survey of the econometric literature is undertaken to determine the duration of cumulative advertising effect on sales. The surveyed studies yield conflicting estimates of the duration interval. The data interval is shown to have a powerful influence on the implied duration of advertising effect. The evidence leads to the conclusion that the cumulative effect of advertising on sales lasts for only months rather than years.

Coffin, Thomas E.

A Pioneering Experiment in Assessing Advertising Effectiveness

Journal of Marketing 27 (3) (July 1963), 1–10.

Co-winner of the 1963 Alpha Kappa Psi Award (as of 1996, the Marketing Science Institute H. Paul Root Award)

According to this article, there are only two basic dimensions to the effectiveness of advertising: (1) size of audience, and (2) depth of impact. The advertising industry has been spending most of its research dollars in measuring the audience component, with the result that we can now measure this dimension reasonably well. Dr. Coffin believes it is now time to spend more dollars in assessing the dimension of impact—for it is this area which, for the future, promises the greatest improvement in advertising evaluation and sound media comparisons.

Desiraju, Ramarao, and Steven M. Shugan
Strategic Service Pricing and Yield Management
Journal of Marketing 63 (1) (January 1999), 44–56.
Co-winner of the 1999 Marketing Science Institute H. Paul Root Award

The authors investigate pricing strategies based on yield management systems (YMS), such as early discounting, overbooking, and limiting early sales, for capacity-constrained services. They find that YMS work best when price-insensitive customers prefer to buy later than price-sensitive consumers. The authors also identify other conditions favoring the use of YMS.

Friestad, Marian, and Peter Wright
The Persuasion Knowledge Model: How People Cope with Persuasion Attempts
Journal of Consumer Research 21 (1) (June 1994), 1–31.
1997 *Journal of Consumer Research* Best Article Award Winner

In theories and studies of persuasion, people's personal knowledge about persuasion agents' goals and tactics, and about how to skillfully cope with these, has been ignored. We present a model of how people develop and use persuasion knowledge to cope with persuasion attempts. We discuss what the model implies about how consumers use marketers' advertising and selling attempts to refine their product attitudes and attitudes toward the marketers themselves. We also explain how this model relates to prior research on consumer behavior and persuasion and what it suggests about the future conduct of consumer research.

Gardner, David M.
Deception in Advertising: A Conceptual Approach
Journal of Marketing 39 (1) (January 1975), 40–6.
1975 Harold H. Maynard Award Winner

By focusing on the interaction of an advertisement with the consumer rather than the act of deceiving, Gardner provides a behavioral definition of deception in advertising that includes three specific categories of deception. An approach to measuring deception from the behavioral perspective is then offered.

Givon, Moshe, and Dan Horsky

Untangling the Effects of Purchase Reinforcement and Advertising Carryover

Marketing Science 9 (2) (Spring 1990), 171–87.

1990 John D. C. Little Award Winner

The dynamic evolvement of market share of a brand in a frequently purchased product category can be driven by two effects, purchase reinforcement, and advertising carryover. The first depends on the actual experience with the brand while the second on the retention of its producer's messages. We present a model to estimate simultaneously the relative magnitude of these two forces. The model also formally treats the issue of temporal aggregation. Our empirical results with several product categories indicate that for monthly and bi-monthly measurement periods, purchase reinforcement dominates carryover of advertising in affecting the evolution of market share.

Gupta, Sunil

Impact of Sales Promotions on When, What, and How Much to Buy

Journal of Marketing Research 25 (4) (November 1988), 342–55.

1993 William F. O'Dell Award Winner

An earlier version of this paper appeared as MSI Report No. 88–108.

The effectiveness of a sales promotion can be examined by decomposing the sales "bump" during the promotion period into sales increase due to brand switching, purchase time acceleration, and stockpiling. The author proposes a method for such a decomposition whereby brand sales are considered the result of consumer decisions about when, what, and how much to buy. The impact of marketing variables on these three consumer decisions is captured by an Erlang-2 interpurchase time model, a multinomial logit model of brand choice, and a cumulative logit model of purchase quantity. The models are estimated with IRI scanner panel data for regular ground coffee. The results indicate that more than 84% of the sales increase due to promotion comes from brand switching (a very small part of which may be switching between different sizes of the same brand). Purchase acceleration in time accounts for less than 14% of the sales increase, whereas stockpiling due to promotion is a negligible phenomenon accounting for less than 2% of the sales increase.

Heilman, Carrie M., Douglas Bowman, and Gordon P. Wright
The Evolution of Brand Preferences and Choice Behaviors of Consumers New to a Market
Journal of Marketing Research 37 (2) (May 2000), 139–55.
2001 Paul E. Green Award Winner

The authors examine how brand preferences and response to marketing activity evolve for consumers new to a market. They develop a theoretical framework that begins with a consumer's first-ever purchase in a product category and describes subsequent purchases as components of sequential purchasing stages. The theory is based on the notion that choices made by consumers new to a market are driven by two competing forces: consumers' desire to collect information about alternatives and their aversion to trying risky ones. These forces give rise to three stages of purchasing: an information collection stage that focuses initially on low-risk, big brand names; a stage in which information collection continues but is extended to lesser-known brands; and a stage of information consolidation leading to preference for the brands that provide the greatest utility. The authors use a logit-mixture model with time-varying parameters to capture the choice dynamics of different consumer segments. The results show the importance of accounting for product experience and learning when studying the dynamic choice processes of consumers new to a market. Insights from this study can help marketers tailor their marketing activities as consumers gain purchasing experience.

Hoch, Stephen J., Xavier Drèze, and Mary E. Purk
EDLP, Hi-Lo, and Margin Arithmetic
Journal of Marketing 58 (4) (October 1994), 16–27.
1994 Alpha Kappa Psi Award Winner (as of 1996, the Marketing Science Institute H. Paul Root Award)

The authors examine the viability of an "everyday low price" (EDLP) strategy in the supermarket grocery industry. In two series of field experiments in 26 product categories conducted in an 86-store grocery chain, they find that a 10% EDLP category price decrease led to a 3% sales volume increase, whereas a 10% Hi-Lo price increase led to a 3% sales decrease. Because consumer demand did not respond much to changes in everyday price, they found large differences in profitability. An EDLP policy reduced profits by 18%, and Hi-Lo pricing increased profits by 15%. In a third study, the authors increase the frequency of shallow price deals in the context of higher everyday prices and find a 3% increase in unit volume and a 4% increase in profit. Finally, they draw a conceptual distinction between "value pricing" at the back door and EDLP pricing at the front door.

Jacobson, Robert, and David A. Aaker

The Strategic Role of Product Quality

Journal of Marketing 51 (4) (October 1987), 31–44.

1987 Alpha Kappa Psi Award Winner (as of 1996, the Marketing Science Institute H. Paul Root Award)

The role of product quality is examined to determine its applicability as a means of gaining a comparative advantage. The authors argue that only by (1) allowing for the possibility of feedback between quality and other strategic factors and (2) controlling for firm-specific effects can the role of quality and key hypotheses be evaluated. Making use of the PIMS data base, the authors detect feedback interactions between product quality and other strategic variables. The findings suggest the importance of product quality and that the successful implementation of a quality strategy can facilitate increased profitability in both a focus and a market share context.

Kivetz, Ran

Promotion Reactance: The Role of Effort-Reward Congruity

Journal of Consumer Research 31 (4) (March 2005), 725–36.

2005 Robert Ferber Award Winner

Incentives may simultaneously entice consumers and arouse reactance. It is proposed that consumers reaffirm their autonomy by choosing rewards that are congruent with the promoted consumption effort (choosing reward *x* over reward *y*, given effort *x*). Such congruity allows consumers to construe their behavior as intrinsically motivated rather than externally induced, because the effort is its own reward. Supporting this conceptualization, the results indicate that preferences for effort-congruent rewards are attenuated among consumers with lower psychological reactance, after a reactance-reduction manipulation, when rewards are independent of personal effort, and when rewards are a by-product rather than the intention of effort.

Krishnamurthi, Lakshman, and S. P. Raj

A Model of Brand Choice and Purchase Quantity Price Sensitivities

Marketing Science 7 (1) (Winter 1988), 1–20.

Co-winner of the 1988 John D. C. Little Award

Many consumer decisions involve a discrete choice and a continuous outcome. Examples of such decisions are whether to own a home or rent one and how much to spend, which brand of orange juice to buy and how many ounces to buy. In cases like these, the choice decision is typically modeled separately, say, using a logit model, and the continuous outcomes modeled separately using regression analysis. However, the continuous outcomes may not be independent of the discrete choice and vice versa, and modeling the two decisions independently can lead to inefficient choice parameter estimates and biased and inconsistent regression parameter estimates. In this paper, we present a methodology from the limited-dependent variable literature to model the dependence between the choice and quantity decisions. Our substantive interest is in the role of price in the choice and quantity decisions. When choosing among alternatives, we argue that consumers consider prices of all the competitive brands. In the quantity decision on the other hand, only the price of the chosen alternative is expected to impact how much of the alternative is purchased. The analysis of three brands, using disaggregate level panel data, strongly supports our hypothesis about the role of competitive prices in the choice and quantity decisions.

Lodish, Leonard M., Magid Abraham, Stuart Kalmenson, Jeanne Livelsberger, Beth Lubetkin, Bruce Richardson, and Mary Ellen Stevens
How T.V. Advertising Works: A Meta-Analysis of 389 Real World Split Cable T.V. Advertising Experiments
Journal of Marketing Research 32 (2) (May 1995), 125–39.
2000 William F. O'Dell Award Winner and 1996 Paul E. Green Award Winner

The authors analyze results of 389 BehaviorScan® matched household, consumer panel, split cable, real world T.V. advertising weight, and copy tests. Additionally, study sponsors—packaged goods advertisers, T.V. networks, and advertising agencies—filled out questionnaires on 140 of the tests, which could test common beliefs about how T.V. advertising works, to evaluate strategic, media, and copy variables unavailable from the BehaviorScan® results. Although some of the variables did indeed identify T.V. advertising that positively affected sales, many of the variables did not differentiate among the sales effects of different advertising treatments. For example, increasing advertising budgets in relation to competitors does not increase sales in general. However, changing brand, copy, and media strategy in categories with many purchase occasions in which in-store merchandising is low increases the likelihood of T.V. advertising positively affecting sales. The authors' data do not show a strong relationship between standard recall and persuasion copy test measures and sales effectiveness. The data also suggest different variable formulations for choice and market response models that include advertising.

Maloney, John C.

Is Advertising Believability Really Important?

Journal of Marketing 27 (4) (October 1963), 1–8.
Co-winner of the 1963 Alpha Kappa Psi Award (as of 1996, the Marketing Science Institute H. Paul Root Award)

Most advertisers feel that to be effective, each advertisement must be noted, understood, and believed. Dr. Maloney draws upon a broad research background to demonstrate that an advertisement can be effective without being completely believed!

Mitra, Anusree, and John G. Lynch, Jr.

Toward a Reconciliation of Market Power and Information Theories of Advertising Effects on Price Elasticity

Journal of Consumer Research 21 (4) (March 1995), 644–59.
1995 Robert Ferber Award Winner

Prior work on the economic effects of advertising has presented conflicting views. Some authors have suggested that advertising creates market power by artificially differentiating brands and thereby lowering price elasticity. Others have viewed advertising as an efficient source of information about the existence of substitutes, arguing that advertising increases price elasticity. The present research proposes a unifying theoretical model in which advertising affects price elasticity through its influence on two mediating constructs: the size of the consideration set and the relative strength of preference. Pretests 1 and 2 examine the effects of advertising on these two constructs. Results from the main experiment show that, in accordance with the theoretical framework, the same advertisements that increased price elasticity in some decision environments decreased it in others.

Moore, Elizabeth S., and Richard J. Lutz

Children, Advertising, and Product Experiences: A Multimethod Inquiry

Journal of Consumer Research 26 (1) (June 2000), 31–48.
Co-winner of the 2003 *Journal of Consumer Research* Best Article Award

Although the prepurchase effects of advertising on children are well documented, little is known about advertising's impact in conjunction with children's product usage experiences. Two studies, one using experimentation and the other using depth interviews, were undertaken to examine this issue. In addition to informational effects, special emphasis was placed on the role affective constructs play in shaping children's impressions. Experimental results indicated that both product trial and advertising have influences, but also that the interplay of these influences differs between older children (10–11-year-olds) and younger children (seven-eight-year-olds). Depth interviews offered further insights into these age differences such that our overall understanding of how older and younger children relate to advertisements and product consumption has been advanced.

Naik, Prasad A., Murali K. Mantrala, and Alan G. Sawyer
Planning Media Schedules in the Presence of Dynamic Advertising Quality
Marketing Science 17 (3) (Summer 1998), 214–35.
1998 Frank M. Bass Dissertation Paper Award Winner

A key task of advertising media planners is to determine the best media schedule of advertising exposures for a certain budget. Conceptually, the planner could choose to do continuous advertising (i.e., schedule ad exposures evenly over all weeks) or follow a strategy of pulsing (i.e., advertise in some weeks of the year and not at other times). Previous theoretical analyses have shown that continuous advertising is optimal for nearly all situations. However, pulsing schedules are very common in practice. Either the practice of pulsing is inappropriate or extant models have not adequately conceptualized the effects of advertising spending over time. This paper offers a model that shows pulsing strategies can generate greater total awareness than the continuous advertising when the effectiveness of advertisement (i.e., ad quality) varies over time. Specifically, ad quality declines because of advertising wearout during periods of continuous advertising and it restores, due to forgetting effects, during periods of no advertising. Such dynamics make it worthwhile for advertisers to stop advertising when ad quality becomes very low and wait for ad quality to restore before starting the next "burst" again, as is common in practice.

Based on the extensive behavioral research on advertising repetition and advertising wearout, we extend the classical Nerlove and Arrow (1962) model by incorporating the notions of repetition wearout, copy wearout, and ad quality restoration. Repetition wearout is a result of excessive frequency because ad viewers perceive that there is nothing new to be gained from processing the ad, they withdraw their attention, or they become unmotivated to react to advertising information. Copy wearout refers to the decline in ad quality due to passage of time independent of the level of frequency. Ad quality restoration is the enhancement of ad quality during media hiatus as a consequence of viewers forgetting the details of the advertised messages, thus making ads appear "like new" when reintroduced later. The proposed model has the property that, when wearout effects are present, a strategy of pulsing is superior to continuous advertising even when the advertising response function is concave. This is illustrated by a numerical example that compares the total awareness generated by a single concentrated pulse of varying duration (blitz schedules) and continuous advertising (the even schedule). This property can be explained by the tension between the pressure to spend the fixed media budget quickly to avoid copy wearout and the opposing pressure to spread out the media spending over time to mitigate repetition wearout.

The proposed model is empirically tested by using brand-level data from two advertising awareness tracking studies that also include the actual spending schedules. The first data set is for a major cereal brand, while the other is for a brand of milk chocolate. Such advertising tracking studies are now a common and popular means for evaluating advertising effectiveness in many markets (e.g., Millward Brown, MarketMind). In the empirical tests, the model parameters are estimated by using the Kalman filter procedure, which is eminently suited for dynamic models because it attends to the intertemporal dependencies in awareness build-up and decay via the use of conditional densities. The estimated parameters are statistically significant, have the expected signs, and are meaningful from both theoretical and managerial viewpoints. The proposed model fits both the data sets rather well and better than several well-known advertising models, namely, the Vidale-Wolfe, Brandaid, Litmus, and Tracker models, but not decisively better than the Nerlove-Arrow model. However, unlike the Nerlove-Arrow model, the proposed model yields different total awareness for different strategies of spending the same fixed budget, thus allowing media planners to discriminate among several media schedules.

Given the empirical support for the model, the paper presents an implementable approach for utilizing it to evaluate large numbers of alternative media schedules and determine the best set of media schedules for consideration in media planning. This approach is based on an algorithm that combines a genetic algorithm with the Kalman filter procedure. The paper presents the results of applying this approach in the case studies of the cereal and milk chocolate brands. The form of the best advertising spending strategies in each case was a pulsing strategy, and there were many schedules that were an improvement over the media schedule actually used in each campaign.

Narasimhan, Chakravarthi
A Price Discrimination Theory of Coupons
Marketing Science 3 (2) (Spring 1984), 128–47.
1984 Best Paper Award Winner (as of 1988, the John D.C. Little Award)

The objective of this paper is to analyze the consumer's decision in electing to use cents-off coupons distributed by manufacturers of consumer products. Arguing that the decision to use coupons is based on the tradeoff between costs of using coupons and the savings obtained, it is shown that coupons can serve as a price discrimination device to provide a lower price to a particular segment of consumers. Based on a price theoretic model, it is shown that the users of coupons are more price elastic than nonusers of coupons and that the opportunity cost of time and other household resource variables are determinant factors in consumers' decisions. Implications derived from the model are tested using diary panel data.

Nordhielm, Christie L.
The Influence of Level of Processing on Advertising Repetition Effects
Journal of Consumer Research 29 (3) (December 2002), 371–82.
2003 Robert Ferber Award Winner

This research examines whether or not repetition of features of a stimulus are subject to wear-out effects that have until now only been tested for the stimulus as a whole. When consumers process features in either a shallower or deeper manner, the level of processing performed dictates the effect of repeated feature exposure on their judgments. When repeated exposures to features are processed in a shallower fashion, there is an enhancement in evaluations with no subsequent downturn, whereas repeated exposure to features that are processed more deeply results in evaluations that exhibit the classic inverted U-shaped pattern.

Obermiller, Carl
Varieties of Mere Exposure: The Effects of Processing Style and Repetition on Affective Response
Journal of Consumer Research 12 (1) (June 1985), 17–30.
1983 Robert Ferber Award Winner

Various theories are examined in order to develop a mechanism that can explain the role of exposure in affective response. Processing style is proposed as a moderating variable that includes attention and elaboration of processing. An experiment suggests that some minimal level of processing (focused attention) may be required for affective response based on sensed familiarity and that more elaborative processing may invoke complex evaluative processes.

Ofek, Elie, and V. Srinivasan
How Much Does the Market Value an Improvement in a Product Attribute?
Marketing Science 21 (4) (Autumn 2002), 398–411.
2002 John D. C. Little Award Winner

A firm contemplating improvements to its product attributes would be interested in the dollar value the market attaches to any potential product modification. In this paper, we derive a measure of market value such that the comparison of the measure against the incremental unit cost of the attribute improvement is key in deciding whether or not the attribute improvement is profitable. Competition from other brands, the potential for market expansion, and heterogeneity in customer preference structures are explicitly modeled using the multinomial logit framework. The analysis yields a closed form expression for the market's value for an attribute improvement (MVAI). A key result we obtain is that customers should be differentially weighted based on their probability of purchasing the firm's product. In particular, customers who exhibit a very high or very low probability of choosing the firm's product should receive less weight in determining MVAI. Because the probability of choice varies across products, the answer to the question of how much the market values an improvement depends on which firm is asking the question. It is shown that customers whose utilities have a greater random component should be weighted less. Furthermore, the measure developed is robust to the influence of outliers in the sample. An empirical illustration of the MVAI measure in the context of a new product development study is provided. The study illustrates the advantages of the proposed measure over currently used approaches and explores the possibility of competitive price reactions.

O'Guinn, Thomas C., and L. J. Shrum
The Role of Television in the Construction of Consumer Reality
Journal of Consumer Research 23 (4) (March 1997), 278–94.
Co-winner of the 2000 *Journal of Consumer Research* Best Article Award

This article presents the results of a two-study inquiry into a particular type of consumer socialization: the construction of consumer social reality via exposure to television. In study 1, estimates of the prevalence of products and activities associated with an affluent lifestyle were positively related to the total amount of television respondents watched. The amount of television viewing was shown to function as a mediating variable between the demographic variables income and education and the affluence estimates. In study 2, which consisted of student participants who were either very heavy or very light soap opera viewers, heavy viewers again provided higher estimates of the prevalence of the same types of products and behaviors measured in study 1. In addition, heavy soap opera viewers constructed their estimates significantly faster than light viewers, which suggests that relevant information is more accessible in memory for heavy viewers than light viewers. The results are consistent with heuristic processing strategies, particularly the availability heuristic, in which individuals infer prevalence from the ease of retrieval of relevant examples (Tversky and Kahneman 1973).

Pechmann, Cornelia, and Susan J. Knight

An Experimental Investigation of the Joint Effects of Advertising and Peers on Adolescents' Beliefs and Intentions about Cigarette Smoking

Journal of Consumer Research 29 (1) (June 2002), 5–19.

2005 *Journal of Consumer Research* Best Article Award Winner

Ninth graders were randomly exposed to one of eight slice-of-life videotapes showing stimulus advertising (cigarette, antismoking, both, neither) and unfamiliar peers who either did or did not smoke cigarettes. The findings indicate that the cigarette advertising primed positive smoker stereotypes, which caused subjects to seek out favorable information about the peers shown smoking. Subjects' beliefs and intentions about cigarette consumption were thereby enhanced by the joint effects of advertising and peers. However, an antismoking advertisement shown in conjunction with cigarette advertising made salient negative smoker stereotypes, evoked unfavorable thoughts about peers shown smoking, and prevented cigarette advertising from promoting smoking.

Politz, Alfred

The Dilemma of Creative Advertising

Journal of Marketing 25 (2) (1960), 1–6.

1960 Alpha Kappa Psi Award Winner (as of 1996, the Marketing Science Institute H. Paul Root Award)

Why does so much of our contemporary advertising violate the rules of effective communication, the application of which could easily increase the power of advertising? This article explains why . . . by pointing out several factors which have been overlooked or misunderstood in advertising theory. It also tells how the advertiser can make his advertising operate much more effectively.

Raju, Jagmohan S., V. Srinivasan, and Rajiv Lal

The Effects of Brand Loyalty on Competitive Price Promotional Strategies

Management Science 36 (3) (March 1990), 276–304.

1991 Frank M. Bass Dissertation Paper Award Winner

This paper analyzes the role played by brand loyalty in determining optimal price promotional strategies used by firms in a competitive setting. (Loyalty is operationalized as the minimum price differential needed before consumers who prefer one brand switch to another brand.) Our objective is to examine how loyalties toward the competing brands influence whether or not firms would use price promotions in a product category. We also examine how loyalty differences lead to variations in the depth and frequency with which price discounts are offered across brands in the same product category. The analysis predicts that a brand's likelihood of using price promotions increases with an increase in the number of competing brands in a product category. In the context of a market in which a brand with a large brand loyalty competes with a brand with a low brand loyalty, it is shown that in equilibrium, the stronger brand (i.e., the brand with the larger loyalty) promotes less frequently than the weaker brand. The results suggest that the weaker brand gains more from price promotions. The analysis helps us understand discounting patterns in markets where store brands, weak national brands, or newly introduced national brands compete against strong, well known, national brands. The findings are based on the unique perfect equilibrium in a finitely repeated game. The predictions of the model are compared with the data on 27 different product categories. The data are consistent with the main findings of the model.

Ritson, Mark, and Richard Elliott
The Social Uses of Advertising: An Ethnographic Study of Adolescent Advertising Audiences
Journal of Consumer Research 26 (3) (December 1999), 260–77.
2000 Robert Ferber Award Winner

Advertising research has focused exclusively on the solitary subject at the expense of understanding the role that advertising plays within the social contexts of group interaction. We develop a number of explanations for this omission before describing the results of an ethnographic study of advertising's contribution to the everyday interactions of adolescent informants at a number of English high schools. The study reveals a series of new, socially related advertising-audience behaviors. Specifically, advertising meanings are shown to possess social uses relating to textual experience, interpretation, evaluation, ritual use, and metaphor. The theoretical and managerial implications of these social uses are then discussed.

Roberts, John H., and James M. Lattin
Development and Testing of a Model of Consideration Set Composition
Journal of Marketing Research 28 (4) (November 1991), 429–40.
1996 William F. O'Dell Award Winner

The authors develop a model of consideration set composition. The approach taken is to compare the marginal expected benefits of including an additional brand in the consideration set with its associated costs of consideration. From an expression of the utility that a brand needs to gain membership in an existing consideration set, the authors derive an expression for set composition and optimal set size. They develop a measurement method to test the model at the individual level and apply it to the ready-to-eat cereal market. The model is tested in two ways. First, the utility function is calibrated at the individual level and the model is used to predict consideration of existing brands. The calibrated model also is used to forecast individual consideration of three new product concepts. Second, the predictive ability of a two-stage model of consideration and choice is tested against a traditional one-stage choice model. The authors conclude with a discussion of management implications of the model in terms of auditing currently available brands and new product management.

Sudhir, K.
Structural Analysis of Manufacturer Pricing in the Presence of a Strategic Retailer
Marketing Science 20 (3) (Summer 2001), 244–64.
2004 Frank M. Bass Dissertation Paper Award Winner

Consumer goods manufacturers usually sell their brands to consumers through common independent retailers. Theoretical research on such channel structures has analyzed the optimal behavior of channel members under alternative assumptions of manufacturer-retailer interaction (Vertical Strategic Interaction). Research in Empirical Industrial Organization has focused on analyzing the competitive interactions between manufacturers (Horizontal Strategic Interaction). Decision support systems have made various assumptions about retailer-pricing rules (e.g., constant markup, category-profit-maximization). The appropriateness of such assumptions about strategic behavior for any specific market, however, is an empirical question. This paper therefore empirically infers (1) the Vertical Strategic Interaction (VSI) between manufacturers and retailer, (2) the Horizontal Strategic Interaction (HSI) between manufacturers simultaneously with the VSI, and (3) the pricing rule used by a retailer.

The approach is particularly appealing because it can be used with widely available scanner data, where there is no information on wholesale prices. Researchers usually have no access to wholesale prices. Even manufacturers, who have access to their own wholesale prices, usually have limited information on competitors' wholesale prices. In the absence of wholesale prices, we derive formulae for wholesale prices using game-theoretic solution techniques under the specific assumptions of vertical and horizontal strategic interaction and retailer-pricing rules. We then embed the formulae for wholesale prices into the estimation equations. While our empirical illustration is using scanner data without wholesale prices, the model itself can be applied when wholesale prices are available.

Early research on the inference of HSI among manufacturers in setting wholesale prices using scanner data (e.g., Kadiyali et al. 1996, 1999) made the simplifying assumption that retailers charge a constant margin. This assumption enabled them to infer wholesale prices and analyze competitive interactions between manufacturers. In this paper, we show that this model is econometrically identical to a model that measures retail-price coordination across brands. Hence, the inferred cooperation among manufacturers could be exaggerated by the coordinated pricing (category management) done by the retailer. We find empirical support for this argument. This highlights the need to properly model and infer VSI simultaneously to accurately estimate the HSI when using data at the retail level. Functional forms of demand have been evaluated in terms of the fit of the model to sales data. But recent theoretical research on channels (Lee and Staelin 1997, Tyagi 1999) has shown that the functional form has serious implications for strategic behavior such as retail passthrough. While the logit and linear model implies equilibrium passthrough of less than 100% (Lee and Staelin call this Vertical Strategic Substitute (VSS)), the multiplicative model implies optimal passthrough of greater than 100% (Vertical Strategic Complement (VSC)). Because passthrough rates on promotions have been found to be below or above 100% (Chevalier and Curhan 1976, Armstrong 1991), we empirically test the appropriateness of the logit (VSS) and the multiplicative (VSC) functional form for the data. We perform our analysis in the yogurt and peanut butter categories for the two biggest stores in a local market.

We find that the VSS implications of the logit fit the data better than the multiplicative model. We also find that for both categories, the best-fitting model is one in which (1) the retailer maximizes category profits, (2) the VSI is Manufacturer-Stackelberg, and (3) manufacturer pricing (HSI) is tacitly collusive. The fact that the retailer maximizes category profits is consistent with theoretical expectations. The inference that the VSI is Manufacturer-Stackelberg reflects the institutional reality of the timing of the game. Retailers set their retail prices after manufacturers set their wholesale prices. Note that in the stores and product categories that we analyze, the two manufacturers own the dominant brands with combined market shares of about 82% in the yogurt market and 65% in the peanut butter market. The result is also consistent with a balance of power argument in the literature. The finding that manufacturer pricing is tacitly collusive is consistent with the argument that firms involved in long-term competition in concentrated markets can achieve tacit collusion. Managers use decision support systems for promotion planning that routinely make assumptions about VSI, HSI, and the functional form. The results from our analysis are of substantive import in judging the appropriateness of assumptions made in such decision support systems.

van Heerde, Harald J., Sachin Gupta, Dick R. Wittink

Is 75% of the Sales Promotion Bump Due to Brand Switching? No, Only 33% Is

Journal of Marketing Research 40 (4) (November 2003), 481–91.

Co-winner of the 2004 Paul E. Green Award

An earlier version of this paper appeared as MSI Report No. 02–116, "The Brand Switching Fraction of Promotion Effects: Unit Sales versus Elasticity Decompositions."

Several researchers have decomposed sales promotion elasticities based on household scanner-panel data. A key result is that the majority of the sales promotion elasticity, approximately 74% on average, is attributed to secondary demand effects (brand switching) and the remainder is attributed to primary demand effects (timing acceleration and quantity increases). The authors demonstrate that this result does not imply that if a brand gains 100 units in sales during a promotion, the other brands in the category lose 74 units. The authors offer a complementary decomposition measure based on unit sales. The measure shows the ratio of the current cross-brand unit sales loss to the current own-brand unit sales gain during promotion; the authors report empirical results for this measure. They also derive analytical expressions that transform the elasticity decomposition into a decomposition of unit sales effects. These expressions show the nature of the difference between the two decompositions. To gain insight into the magnitude of the difference, the authors apply these expressions to previously reported elasticity decomposition results and find that approximately 33% of the unit sales increase is attributable to losses incurred by other brands in the same category.

White, Irving S.

The Functions of Advertising in Our Culture

Journal of Marketing 24 (1) (July 1959), 8–14.

1959 Alpha Kappa Psi Award Winner (as of 1996, the Marketing Science Institute H. Paul Root Award)

What are advertising's limits and potentialities? The author shows how three major variables in the communication process between advertising and the consumer—cultural attitudes; brand imagery; and direct experience with a product—are related to advertising effectiveness.

Wind, Yoram, and Henry J. Claycamp

Planning Product Line Strategy: A Matrix Approach

Journal of Marketing 40 (1) (January 1976), 2–9.

1976 Alpha Kappa Psi Award Winner (as of 1996, the Marketing Science Institute H. Paul Root Award)

The authors propose a five-step approach to product line planning. The approach centers around the product evaluation matrix, which provides an integrative framework for measuring and monitoring actual and anticipated product performance in terms of "hard" data on sales, profits, and market share.

Xie, Jinhong, and Steven M. Shugan

Electronic Tickets, Smart Cards, and Online Prepayments: When and How to Advance Sell

Marketing Science 20 (3) (Summer 2001), 219–43.

Co-winner of the 2001 John D. C. Little Award

Advance selling occurs when sellers allow buyers to purchase at a time preceding consumption (Shugan and Xie 2000). Electronic tickets, smart cards, online prepayments, and other technological advances make advance selling possible for many, if not all, service providers. These technologies lower the cost of making complex transactions at a greater distance from the seller's site. They also give sellers more control over advance selling by decreasing arbitrage. As technology enhances the capability to advance sell, more academic attention is vital. This paper strives to exploit these technologies by developing advance-selling strategies. Until recently, advance-selling research focused on the airline industry and specific characteristics of that industry. These characteristics included the price insensitivity of late arrivals (e.g., business travelers) compared with early arrivals (e.g., leisure travelers), demand uncertainty across flights on the same day, and capacity constraints.

Recent findings by Shugan and Xie (2000) show that advance selling is a far more general marketing tool than previously thought. It does not require these industry-specific characteristics. It only requires the existence of buyer uncertainty about future valuations. Moreover, sellers without the ability to price discriminate can use advance selling to improve profits to the level of first-degree price discrimination. This finding is important because buyers are nearly always uncertain about their future valuations for most services (e.g., the utility of next year's vacation or a future college education). In this paper, we take the next step from Shugan and Xie (2000). We show that advance-selling profits do not come from buyer surplus, but from more buyers being able to purchase. We determine when and how to advance sell in a variety of situations, including situations with limited capacity, second-period arrivals, refunds, buyer risk aversion, exogenous credibility, continuous preference distributions, and premium pricing. We determine when advance selling improves profits and, when it does, how to set advance prices. We ask and answer seven questions. First, when should sellers advance sell? Second, how much can advance selling improve profits compared with only spot selling? Third, what factors impact the profitability of advance selling and how? Fourth, should advance prices be higher or lower or the same as spot prices? Fifth, how do capacity constraints impact advance-selling strategies? Sixth, should sellers limit the number of advance sales? Finally, what is the possible impact of buyer risk aversion?

First, we provide precise conditions when sellers should advance sell. For example, without capacity constraints, we show that sellers should advance sell when marginal costs are sufficiently low to make it profitable to sell to buyers with low valuations and sufficiently high to convince buyers that the spot price will be higher than the advance price. Second, we find that advance selling can almost double the profits from optimal spot selling to early arrivals. We also show that advance selling has no impact on consumer surplus in markets with homogenous consumers and no capacity constraints. Therefore, advance selling can increase social welfare because seller profits increase. Third, we find that two very important factors impacting the profitability of advance selling are seller credibility and marginal costs. Buyers only advance buy when they expect an advantage from advance buying over spot buying. Without capacity constraints, sellers must credibly convince buyers that the advance price is at a discount to the spot price. We show that this condition is met under different circumstances. For example, large marginal costs can create credibility because buyers believe that these costs will lead to high spot prices. Fourth, we find (although optimal advance prices can be at a discount to the spot price) that sometimes a premium is optimal. Premiums are optimal when capacity is large (but limited) and marginal costs are not too large. Buyers advance purchase at a premium to spot prices when capacity is limited and spot prices are low. (Note that this is not a risk premium, and risk aversion is not required.) No prior research has suggested this strategy because that research relies on the assumption that early arrivals are more price sensitive than later ones. Without that assumption, premium advance pricing is sometimes optimal.

Fifth, we find that binding capacity constraints can impact the profitability of advance selling in opposite ways. On one hand, capacity constraints create seller credibility. Buyers believe that spot prices will be high when they know spot capacity is limited (and, perhaps, more limited by advance sales). On the other hand, when capacity is limited, the need to increase sales from discounted advance prices diminishes. Sixth, consistent with Desiraju and Shugan (1999) we find that limiting advance sales can be profitable, but only under restrictive conditions. These conditions are:

(1) selling to all early arrivals would leave insufficient capacity in the spot period to sell to all second-period arrivals with high valuations, (2) the optimal spot price is high, and (3) marginal costs are sufficiently small to make advance selling profitable. Finally, we find that buyer risk aversion can sometimes increase the profitability of advance selling. Our findings provide precise guidelines for a large number of service providers that will have the technical capability to advance sell. For those service providers, advance selling provides a creative pricing strategy that can potentially provide substantial improvements in profits.

Zeithaml, Valarie A.

Consumer Response to In-Store Price Information Environments

Journal of Consumer Research 8 (4) (March 1982), 357–69.
1981 Robert Ferber Award Winner

A laboratory experiment evaluated the impact of eight in-store information environments on consumer processing of price information. Results reveal that the format of information provision significantly affected subjects' cognitive, affective, and behavioral responses. Findings suggest that both item marking and a list of unit prices facilitate processing of grocery-store prices.

Zeithaml, Valarie A.

Consumer Perceptions of Price, Quality, and Value: A Means-End Model and Synthesis of Evidence

Journal of Marketing 52 (3) (July 1988), 2–22.
1988 Harold H. Maynard Award Winner
An earlier version of this paper appeared as MSI Report No. 87–101, "Defining and Relating Price, Perceived Quality, and Perceived Value."

Evidence from past research and insights from an exploratory investigation are combined in a conceptual model that defines and relates price, perceived quality, and perceived value. Propositions about the concepts and their relationships are presented, then supported with evidence from the literature. Discussion centers on directions for research and implications for managing price, quality, and value.

Additional Relevant Papers: Marketing Mix

Ansari, Asim, and Carl F. Mela

E-Customization

Journal of Marketing Research 40 (2) (May 2003), 131–45. See page 54 for abstract.

Co-winner of the 2004 Paul E. Green Award

Bass, Frank M.

The Theory of Stochastic Preference and Brand Switching

Journal of Marketing Research 11 (1) (February 1974), 1–20. See page 148 for abstract.

Co-winner of the 1979 William F. O'Dell Award

Bult, Jan Roelf, and Tom Wansbeek

Optimal Selection for Direct Mail

Marketing Science 14 (4) (Autumn 1995), 378–94. See page 55 for abstract.

1995 Frank M. Bass Dissertation Paper Award Winner

Dean, Joel

Does Advertising Belong in the Capital Budget?

Journal of Marketing 30 (4) (October 1966), 15–21. See page 39 for abstract.

1966 Alpha Kappa Psi Award Winner (as of 1996, the Marketing Science Institute H. Paul Root Award)

Dekimpe, Marnik G., and Dominique M. Hanssens

Sustained Spending and Persistent Response: A New Look at Long-Term Marketing Profitability

Journal of Marketing Research 36 (4) (November 1999), 397–412. See page 40 for abstract.

2000 Paul E. Green Award Winner

Fader, Peter S., and Bruce G. S. Hardie

Modeling Consumer Choice among SKUs

Journal of Marketing Research 33 (4) (November 1996), 442–52. See page 91 for abstract.

1997 Paul E. Green Award Winner

Jacobson, Robert, and David A. Aaker

Is Market Share All That It's Cracked Up to Be?

Journal of Marketing 49 (4) (Fall 1985), 11–22. See page 40 for abstract.

1985 Alpha Kappa Psi Award Winner (as of 1996, the Marketing Science Institute H. Paul Root Award)

McAlister, Leigh

Choosing Multiple Items from a Product Class

Journal of Consumer Research 6 (3) (December 1979), 213–24. See page 156 for abstract.

1978 Robert Ferber Award Winner

McCracken, Grant

Culture and Consumption: A Theoretical Account of the Structure and Movement of the Cultural Meaning of Consumer Goods

Journal of Consumer Research 13 (1) (June 1986), 71–84. See page 156 for abstract.

1987 Association for Consumer Research Best Article Award Winner (as of 1996, the *Journal of Consumer Research* Best Article Award Winner)

Raju, Jagmohan S., Raj Sethuraman, and Sanjay K. Dhar

The Introduction and Performance of Store Brands

Management Science 41 (6) (June 1995), 957–78. See page 31 for abstract.

Co-winner of the 1995 John D. C. Little Award

Stremersch, Stefan, and Gerard J. Tellis

Strategic Bundling of Products and Prices: A New Synthesis for Marketing

Journal of Marketing 66 (1) (January 2002), 55–72. See page 186 for abstract.

2002 Harold H. Maynard Award Winner

8

Customer Insight

Early in the development of customer insight research, Jacoby (1978) pointed to problems with existing work and encouraged researchers to find new models and methods. One of the resulting streams of customer insight research has as its objective predicting unexpected consumer choices. This stream has explored the impact of variety-seeking behavior, decision rules and heuristics, choice context, and social context. Two additional streams focus on the processes that underlie choice. Of those, one focuses on learning and cognition (perception, memory, judging, thinking, etc.), and a second focuses on affect and emotion. The final stream of customer insight research considers the relationships between culture and consumption.

Consumer Choice

Citing the fact that a consumer does not choose the same brand on every occasion, Bass (1974) stated, *"It will never be possible to provide good predictions of individual consumer choice behavior for separate choice occasions"* (p. 19; italics are in original). As an alternative to deterministic models of consumer choice, he proposed a simple and elegant probabilistic model which, given a set of competitive brands' market shares, provides reasonable predictions of the percentage of consumers that will switch between each pair of brands. Two streams of research can be thought of as emerging from his work. First, there are prize-winning stochastic models that are described in Chapter 7, "Marketing Mix." Second, there are prize-winning papers that focus on explaining why a consumer might buy different brands on different occasions. These papers consider consumers' variety-seeking behavior, consumers' use of decision rules and heuristics, the impact of the choice context, and the impact of the social context.

Variety-seeking Behavior

McAlister (1979) suggested that a consumer's choice history could influence that consumer's current choice. Her model assumes that a consumer becomes satiated with an attribute provided by recently consumed brands, thereby causing other brands, rich in different attributes, to become more attractive.

Decision Rules and Heuristics

Several researchers have explored the impact of the consumers' decision rules and heuristics on a target brand's choice share in different environments. Simonson (1989) proposed that consumers choose the alternative that is supported by the best reasons and held that both the attraction effect and the compromise effect could be explained as consequences of consumers making choices based on good reasons. In the first case, he argued that introducing a dominated alternative into a choice set increases choice share for the dominating alternative because dominance is a good reason for choice; in the second, he argued that introducing a third alternative into a two-alternative set so that one of the original alternatives becomes a compromise alternative increases choice share for the compromise alternative because compromise is a good reason for choice.

Simonson (1989) also argued that asking a decision maker to provide reasons for his or her choice causes the decision maker to launch a search for an acceptable rationale; Briley, Morris, and Simonson (2000) extended that work to show that the knowledge that the decision maker draws upon to develop reasons is culturally rooted. When asked to give reasons for their choices, people from East Asian cultures grow more likely to compromise while people from North American culture grow less likely to compromise. Simonson and Tversky (1992) generalized the reason-based choice model by hypothesizing two effects that can account for attraction, compromise, and many other phenomena. Those two effects are tradeoff contrast (the extent to which tradeoffs among other options in the choice set favor the target brand) and extremeness aversion (target brand becomes more attractive when it is seen as a compromise alternative).

Choice Context

Puto (1987) and Lurie (2004) suggested that choice context influences a consumer's choice. Puto suggested that elements of the choice context could influence the reference point against which decision alternatives are evaluated. This change in the reference point, which can be influenced by marketing interventions, can cause a consumer to choose a different brand. Lurie considered the problem of information overload in consumer choice and suggested that existing measures that summarize the amount of information in a set of choice alternatives should be extended beyond number of attributes and number of alternatives to also consider the number of attribute levels and the distribution of those levels across alternatives. He showed how information structure influences the pattern of information acquired and, ultimately, decision quality.

Social Context

Frenzen and Davis (1990) showed that going beyond an understanding of the consumer to also consider the consumer's social network can improve our ability to predict consumer choice. Building on social network research as presented in Brown and Reingen (1987), Frenzen and Davis studied the home party method of direct sales and found that consumers' preferences for characteristics of the products explained only 31% of the variance in purchase decisions, while the strength of the ties between the consumers and seller explained 66% of that variance. Frenzen and Nakamoto (1993) showed that we can understand a consumer's decision to pass along information better if we expand the focus from the social network to also include the consumer's judgment of the moral hazard associated with the information they might pass along.

Cognition and Learning

In one of the earliest prize-winning papers, Bayton (1958) urged consumer behavior researchers to go beyond motivational research to also consider cognition (perception, memory, judging, thinking, etc.) and learning. Bettman (1979) provided a road map for research into those topics with a review of psychological research on human memory in which he illustrated the applicability of that research to marketing. He argued that it was important to discover what information consumers retain in memory and how available external memory, time pressure, and memory structure affect the use of that information.

Consumer Expertise

Alba and Hutchinson (1987) laid the foundation for research on consumer knowledge, identifying five dimensions of expertise: cognitive effort, cognitive structure, analysis, elaboration, and memory. Alba and Hutchinson (2000) extended their framework by adding a metacognitive dimension, arguing that consumers are frequently mistaken about the reliability of their memories, and that this affects assessment of the validity of their beliefs and the accuracy of their forecasts. Rao and Monroe (1988) showed that consumers moderately familiar with a category are least likely to use price as an indicator of quality. Consumers who are more familiar use price as an indicaton of quality based on their knowledge, whereas consumers who are less familiar use price as an indicator of quality based on their beliefs.

Lynch, Chakravarti, and Mitra (1991) showed that although contrast effects may change attribute ratings, these do not always reflect true changes in consumers' mental representations. Changes in preference rank orders are more definitive evidence of true changes. Contrast effects on ratings are more likely to imply true mental representation changes for low-knowledge consumers. For high-knowledge consumers, such changes may only represent how they used the scale.

Research asserting that the main advantage experts have over novices is their ability to impose structure in ambiguous situations led Brucks (1985) to realize that a predominating data collection paradigm of the time—the information display board—was likely to wash out expertise effects. She tested the basic theory by developing a new experimental method that could capture the effect of expertise in ill-structured decisions and found that expertise both facilitates search and makes it more efficient when the decision problem is complex and ill-structured.

Memory-based Decisions

Lynch, Marmorstein, and Weigold (1988) studied choice that is memory based or mixed rather than just stimulus based. They investigated conditions that cause consumers to choose by affect referral rather than by a multiattribute comparison. Considering memory-based judgments, Chattopadhyay and Alba (1988) investigated the link between advertising message recall and attitude. They show that over time, abstract cognitive responses are strong predictors of attitude.

Learning Preferences

Hoch and Deighton (1989) showed that learning from personal experience with a product is not a simple process and does not necessarily result in the consumer's grasping an objective truth. They identified three influences on learning: the consumer's familiarity with the product category, the consumer's motivation to learn, and the degree to which information is ambiguous. Huffman and Houston (1993) suggested that the consumer's goal also influences what the consumer learns because the goal helps the consumer organize the knowledge gained through experience. West (1996) considered the problem consumers face when trying to learn the preferences of others. She shows that when feedback is provided, consumers move beyond the naive assumption that others' preferences are like their own.

Affect and Emotion

As consumer behavior researchers began to study the relationship between emotions and consumers' decisions, they realized that the emotion measurement scales they brought over from psychology did not capture the full range of emotions associated with consumption. Richins (1997) developed the CES (Consumption Emotion Scale) to address those limitations.

Luce (1998) and Adaval (2001) looked at the impact of emotions on consumers' decision-making processes. Luce showed that consumers cope with decision-generated negative emotion by using avoidant options: choosing the status quo option, choosing a dominant option, and prolonged search. Adaval showed that mood-consistent product information is given more salience in a decision when the consumer bases evaluations on hedonic criteria.

Culture and Consumption

In one of the earliest prize-winning papers, Martineau (1958) made the point that consumption patterns operate as prestige symbols to define class membership. Elaborating on this theme, McCracken (1986) suggested that cultural meaning in a consumer society flows from the culturally constituted world to consumer goods via advertising and the fashion system and from consumer goods to consumers via consumers' possession, exchange, grooming, and divestment rituals. Kleine and Kernan (1991) offered a social-psychological method for studying the process by which context influences the meaning that a consumer ascribes to an object. Using that method, they provided evidence consistent with McCracken's contention that, through advertising ". . . virtually any product can take virtually any meaning" (McCracken 1986, p. 314). Consistent with McCracken's contention that cultural meaning flows continually among the culturally constituted world, consumer goods, and individual consumers, Belk, Wallendorf, and Sherry (1989) focused on the sacrilization of the secular. They documented and described the properties and manifestations of sacredness that consumers invest in consumption.

Sirsi, Ward, and Reingen (1996) considered the link between culture and consumption by investigating causal reasoning. They found that experts share core concepts about culturally salient products and that novices share a few of those concepts about the most salient products. While reasoning that links core concepts was generally shared in the culture, reasoning that linked more than two noncore concepts was virtually unique to the individual, even across experts.

Research Priorities

MSI member companies articulate their need for deeper customer insights by describing the issues that those insights would help them address, whether the insights result from studying choice, cognition, learning, affect, emotion, culture, consumption, or some other phenomenon. In roughly decreasing order of importance, those issues are:

- consumer behavior through the consumer's life phases, understanding of which would let companies better anticipate emerging consumer needs
- brand equity (how consumers store and use information about brands)
- the impact of marketing programs (marketing mix, advertisements, customer experiences, nonverbal brand elements, corporate logos, etc.) on brand equity and how that impact changes during the course of the product life cycle
- the impact of brand personality dimensions on brand equity and whether that impact differs depending on the objective (trial, preference, loyalty, etc.) and for different product categories
- the new product or service adoption process
- whether there is communication synergy across communication media and, if so, what drives that synergy
- consumers' reactions to nontraditional media (product placements, sponsorships, "buzz" marketing, in-store marketing, etc.)
- the psychological aspects of pricing and how one can influence price perceptions and evaluations
- marketing to special populations (teens, ethnic groups, developing markets, etc.)

Abstracts: Customer Insight

Adaval, Rashmi

Sometimes It Just Feels Right: The Differential Weighting of Affect-Consistent and Affect-Inconsistent Product Information

Journal of Consumer Research 28 (1) (June 2001), 1–17.
2002 Robert Ferber Award Winner

An affect-confirmation process is proposed to explain the conditions in which information that is similar in valence (i.e., evaluatively consistent) with a person's mood is weighted more heavily in product judgments. Specifically, the affect that participants experience as a result of a transitory mood state may appear to either confirm or disconfirm their reactions to product information, leading them to give this information more or less weight when evaluating the product as a whole. This affective confirmation typically occurs when hedonic criteria are considered more important in evaluation than utilitarian criteria. Four experiments confirmed implications of this conceptualization.

Alba, Joseph W., and J. Wesley Hutchinson

Dimensions of Consumer Expertise

Journal of Consumer Research 13 (4) (March 1987), 411–54.
1988 Association for Consumer Research Best Article Award Winner (as of 1996, the *Journal of Consumer Research* Best Article Award Winner)

The purpose of this article is to review basic empirical results from the psychological literature in a way that provides a useful foundation for research on consumer knowledge. A conceptual organization for this diverse literature is provided by two fundamental distinctions. First, consumer expertise is distinguished from product-related experience. Second, five distinct aspects, or dimensions, of expertise are identified: cognitive effort, cognitive structure, analysis, elaboration, and memory. Improvements in the first two dimensions are shown to have general beneficial effects on the latter three. Analysis, elaboration, and memory are shown to have more specific interrelationships. The empirical findings related to each dimension are reviewed and, on the basis of those findings, specific research hypotheses about the effects of expertise on consumer behavior are suggested.

Alba, Joseph W., and J. Wesley Hutchinson
Knowledge Calibration: What Consumers Know and What They Think They Know
Journal of Consumer Research 26 (2) (September 2000), 123–56.
Co-winner of the 2003 *Journal of Consumer Research* Best Article Award

Consumer knowledge is seldom complete or errorless. Therefore, the self-assessed validity of knowledge and consequent knowledge calibration (i.e., the correspondence between self-assessed and actual validity) is an important issue for the study of consumer decision making. In this article we describe methods and models used in calibration research. We then review a wide variety of empirical results indicating that high levels of calibration are achieved rarely, moderate levels that include some degree of systematic bias are the norm, and confidence and accuracy are sometimes completely uncorrelated. Finally, we examine the explanations of miscalibration and offer suggestions for future research.

Bass, Frank M.
The Theory of Stochastic Preference and Brand Switching
Journal of Marketing Research 11 (1) (February 1974), 1–20.
Co-winner of the 1979 William F. O'Dell Award

Strong evidence will be introduced which suggests that brand choice behavior is substantially stochastic. A general theory of stochastic preference is presented and tested. Brand switching data are shown to be in substantial agreement with the theory.

Bayton, James A.
Motivation, Cognition, Learning: Basic Factors in Consumer Behavior
Journal of Marketing 22 (3) (January 1958), 282–89.
1957 Alpha Kappa Psi Award Winner (as of 1996, the Marketing Science Institute H. Paul Root Award)

This is a comprehensive application of contemporary psychological theories to the analysis of consumer behavior. Although modern marketing is drawing heavily upon psychology, there is a tendency for the emphasis to become somewhat "one-sided," as observed in the stress on motivation research. The danger is that concentration upon only one aspect of behavior will obscure other important psychological dimensions necessary to understanding the behavior of consumers.

Belk, Russell W., Melanie Wallendorf, and John F. Sherry, Jr.

The Sacred and the Profane in Consumer Behavior: Theodicy on the Odyssey

Journal of Consumer Research 16 (1) (June 1989), 1–38.

1992 Association for Consumer Research Best Article Award Winner (as of 1996, the *Journal of Consumer Research* Best Article Award Winner)

Two processes at work in contemporary society are the secularization of religion and the sacralization of the secular. Consumer behavior shapes and reflects these processes. For many, consumption has become a vehicle for experiencing the sacred. This article explores the ritual substratum of consumption and describes properties and manifestations of the sacred inherent in consumer behavior. Similarly, the processes by which consumers sacralize and desacralize dimensions of their experience are described. The naturalistic inquiry approach driving the insights in this article is advanced as a corrective to a premature narrowing of focus in consumer research.

Bettman, James R.

Memory Factors in Consumer Choice: A Review

Journal of Marketing 43 (2) (Spring 1979), 37–53.

1979 Harold H. Maynard Award Winner

This paper reviews research and theory on human memory, emphasizing key findings and concepts of importance to marketing and consumer choice. Several implications for promotional decisions are discussed. It is hoped that this review will stimulate further research on, and applications of, memory principles in marketing.

Briley, Donnel A., Michael W. Morris, and Itamar Simonson

Reasons as Carriers of Culture: Dynamic versus Dispositional Models of Cultural Influence on Decision Making

Journal of Consumer Research 27 (2) (September 2000), 157–78.

Co-winner of the 2001 Robert Ferber Award

We argue that a way culture influences decisions is through the reasons that individuals recruit when required to explain their choices. Specifically, we propose that cultures endow individuals with different rules or principles that provide guidance for making decisions, and a need to provide reasons activates such cultural knowledge. This proposition, representing a dynamic rather than dispositional view of cultural influence, is investigated in studies of consumer decisions that involve a trade-off between diverging attributes, such as low price and high quality. Principles enjoining compromise are more salient in East Asian cultures than in North American culture, and accordingly, we predict that cultural differences in the tendency to choose compromise options will be greater when the decision task requires that participants provide reasons. In study 1, a difference between Hong Kong Chinese and North American participants in the tendency to select compromise products emerged only when they were asked to explain their decisions, with Hong Kong decision makers more likely and Americans less likely to compromise. Content analysis of participants' reasons confirmed that cultural differences in the frequency of generating particular types of reasons mediated the difference in choices. Studies 2 and 3 replicate the interactive effect of culture and the need to provide reasons in a comparison of North American versus Japanese participants and in a comparison of European-American and Asian-American participants, respectively. Studies 4 and 5 found that Hong Kong Chinese participants, compared with Americans, evaluate proverbs and the reasons of others more positively when these favor compromise. We discuss the value of conceptualizing cultural influences in terms of dynamic strategies rather than as dispositional tendencies.

Brown, Jacqueline Johnson, and Peter H. Reingen
Social Ties and Word-of-Mouth Referral Behavior
Journal of Consumer Research 14 (3) (December 1987), 350–62.
1988 Robert Ferber Award Winner

This article presents a network analysis of word-of-mouth referral behavior in a natural environment. The relational properties of tie strength and homophily were employed to examine referral behavior at micro and macro levels of inquiry. The study demonstrates different roles played by weak and strong social ties. At the macro level, weak ties displayed an important bridging function, allowing information to travel from one distinct subgroup of referral actors to another subgroup in the broader social system. At the micro level, strong and homophilous ties were more likely to be activated for the flow of referral information. Strong ties were also perceived as more influential than weak ties, and they were more likely to be utilized as sources of information for related goods.

Brucks, Merrie
The Effects of Product Class Knowledge on Information Search Behavior
Journal of Consumer Research 12 (1) (June 1985), 1–16.
1984 Robert Ferber Award Winner

The effects of prior knowledge about a product class on various characteristics of pre-purchase information search within that product class are examined. A new search task methodology is used that imposes only a limited amount of structure on the search task: subjects are not cued with a list of attributes, and the problem is not structured in a brand-by-attribute matrix. The results indicate that prior knowledge facilitates the acquisition of new information and increases search efficiency. The results also support the conceptual distinction between objective and subjective knowledge.

Chattopadhyay, Amitava, and Joseph W. Alba
The Situational Importance of Recall and Inference in Consumer Decision Making
Journal of Consumer Research 15 (1) (June 1988), 1–12.
Co-winner of the 1987 Robert Ferber Award

A version of this paper (published in 1989) appeared as MSI Report No. 89–103, "The Relationship Between Recall, Cognitive Responses, and Advertising Effectiveness: Effects of Delay and Context."

An experiment, which examines the relationship between cognition and attitude toward a product as a function of time and the presence of information about a competing product, is described. A scheme, which partitions cognitive responses into categories on the basis of their relative abstractness and, therefore, memorability, is proposed. Results show that the proposed scheme accounts for a significant amount of attitude variance and outperforms the traditional cognitive response scheme, especially after a delay. Results also show that, contrary to recent theory and research regarding the lack of correlation between attitude and recall, recall can be a predictor of attitude given the proper context and a theoretically justifiable recall measure.

Frenzen, Jonathan K., and Harry L. Davis
Purchasing Behavior in Embedded Markets
Journal of Consumer Research 17 (1) (June 1990), 1–12.
1991 Robert Ferber Award Winner

This article explores the concept of market embeddedness and its impact on purchasing behavior in a consumer market. Embeddedness exists when consumers derive utility from two sources simultaneously: from attributes of the product and from social capital found in preexisting ties between buyers and sellers. This framework is applied to the home party method of direct sales. We find that the degree of social capital present, as measured by the strength of the buyer-seller tie and buyer indebtedness to the seller, significantly affects the likelihood of purchase.

Frenzen, Jonathan, and Kent Nakamoto
Structure, Cooperation, and the Flow of Market Information
Journal of Consumer Research 20 (3) (December 1993), 360–75.
1996 *Journal of Consumer Research* Best Article Award Winner

This article explores the potential impact of individual consumer decisions to transmit or withhold word-of-mouth information on the flow of information in a market. Information flow is examined in networks composed of graphs and nodes, where graphs represent channels that foster information flow and nodes represent sentient decision makers who can potentially impede or foster information flow. We assert that actors in embedded markets first judge the moral hazards imposed by the information they consider for transmission and the social context of transmission, and then moderate their decisions to transmit the information in light of these judgments. We analyze this process using a modified version of Marshall Sahlins's social exchange theory, examine the plausibility of this analysis using two laboratory experiments, and explore the consequences of this behavior at the aggregate level using a computer simulation. Our view highlights the importance of the interplay of individuals and their social context for understanding word-of-mouth processes.

Hoch, Stephen J., and John Deighton
Managing What Consumers Learn from Experience
Journal of Marketing 53 (2) (April 1989), 1–20.
1989 Alpha Kappa Psi Award Winner (as of 1996, the Marketing Science Institute H. Paul Root Award)

The authors argue that what consumers learn from the experience of using products is not a simple matter of discovering objective truth. They frame the problem of learning from experience as a four stage process (hypothesizing-exposure-encoding-integration) with three moderating factors (familiarity with the domain, motivation to learn, and the ambiguity of the information environment). The framework is used to identify where learning from product consumption experience is most open to managerial influence. The authors discuss strategic tools for managing experiential learning and consider applications to the simulation of learning in concept and pre-test-market product testing.

Huffman, Cynthia, and Michael J. Houston

Goal-Oriented Experiences and the Development of Knowledge

Journal of Consumer Research 20 (2) (September 1993), 190–207.

1994 Robert Ferber Award Winner

This research investigates the learning that occurs throughout several information acquisition and choice experiences. The effects of three factors that may naturally vary in consumer experiences are studied: a consumer's goals, how much the consumer knows about the product's features prior to information acquisition and choice, and the content of feedback received after choice. Results show that the information consumers learn is organized in memory around the goal(s) that drives the experiences. Further, higher levels of prior feature knowledge result in more accurate knowledge after experience, but, contrary to predictions, subjects with no prior feature knowledge are quite adept at focusing on their goal in the choice process and at learning goal-appropriate information. The presence of feedback and its consistency with a consumer's goal are also shown to affect the goal orientation and organization of brand and feature knowledge gained during choice experiences.

Jacoby, Jacob

Consumer Research: A State of the Art Review

Journal of Marketing 42 (2) (April 1978), 87–96.

1978 Harold H. Maynard Award Winner

This author finds much of current theory and methodology lacking in fundamental research—strong medicine!

Kleine, Robert E., III, and Jerome B. Kernan

Contextual Influences on the Meanings Ascribed to Ordinary Consumption Objects

Journal of Consumer Research 18 (3) (December 1991), 311–24.

1992 Robert Ferber Award Winner

Although the perception of contextualized objects pervades our everyday experiences, the literature provides little insight into how consumers ascribe meaning to contextualized products, or indeed into what meaning is. We address this gap in the literature by providing a conceptualization of consumption-object meaning and an a priori model for measuring it. An experiment tested several hypotheses concerning how the kind and amount of context affects the meanings people ascribe to ordinary consumption objects (and the labels that they use to identify those meanings). Overall, the findings support the proposed conceptualization.

Luce, Mary Frances

Choosing to Avoid: Coping with Negatively Emotion-Laden Consumer Decisions

Journal of Consumer Research 24 (4) (March 1998), 409–33.

1998 Robert Ferber Award Winner

This article addresses how consumers resolve decisions involving conflict between attributes linked to highly valued goals, such as an automobile purchase decision requiring determination of how much safety one is willing to sacrifice in order to obtain other benefits. One salient goal for these decisions may be coping with or minimizing the negative emotion generated during decision making. The conceptual framework developed in this article predicts that choosing avoidant options (e.g., the option to maintain the status quo) can satisfy coping goals by minimizing explicit confrontation of negative potential decision consequences and difficult trade-offs. Two experiments demonstrate that reported emotion can be altered by manipulating decision attributes, that the opportunity to choose an avoidant option mitigates levels of reported emotion, and that increasingly emotion-laden decision environments are associated with more choice of avoidant options. Mediation analyses indicate that actual choice of an avoidant option results in less retrospective negative emotion (in experiment 1) and that increased initial negative emotion results in increased choice of avoidant options (in experiment 2). Mediation analyses for experiment 2 also indicate that increased response times mediate avoidant choice, in contrast to explanations of the status quo bias and similar choice phenomena that appeal to decision makers' desires to minimize cognitive effort.

Lurie, Nicholas H.

Decision Making in Information-Rich Environments: The Role of Information Structure

Journal of Consumer Research 30 (4) (March 2004), 473–86.

2004 Robert Ferber Award Winner

Today's consumers are often overloaded with information. This article argues that traditional approaches to measuring the amount of information in a choice set fail to account for important structural dimensions of information and may therefore incorrectly predict information overload. Two experiments show that a structural approach to measuring information, such as information theory, is better able to predict information overload and that information structure also has important implications for information acquisition. A Monte Carlo simulation, in which decision rules are applied to multiple information environments, shows that the amount of information processing mediates the relationship between information structure and information overload.

Lynch, John G., Jr., Dipankar Chakravarti, and Anusree Mitra

Contrast Effects in Consumer Judgments: Changes in Mental Representations or in the Anchoring of Rating Scales?

Journal of Consumer Research 18 (3) (December 1991), 284–97.

1994 Association for Consumer Research Best Article Award Winner (as of 1996, the *Journal of Consumer Research* Best Article Award Winner)

Contrast effects in consumers' judgments of products can stem from changes in how consumers mentally represent the stimuli or in how they anchor rating scales when mapping context-invariant mental representations onto those scales. We present a framework for distinguishing between these types of contrast effects on the basis of whether changes in mean ratings of multiattribute stimuli are accompanied by evidence of changes in their rank order. We also report two empirical studies. In study 1, mean overall ratings of a "core set" of car profiles showed contrast effects due to manipulations of the ranges of gas mileage and price in several sets of "context profiles." Diagnostic tests implied that these effects reflected changes in response-scale anchoring rather than in mental representations. In study 2, consumers high and low in knowledge of automobile prices showed equally large contrast effects on ratings of the expensiveness of a core set of real cars. Diagnostic tests showed that these reflected true changes in mental representation for low-knowledge consumers but only changes in scale anchoring for more knowledgeable ones. Thus, ostensibly similar context effects on simple ratings have different underlying causes and implications for behavior. The findings suggest alternative interpretations of contrast effects in past research on price perception, consumer satisfaction, and service quality.

Lynch, John G., Jr., Howard Marmorstein, and Michael F. Weigold

Choices from Sets Including Remembered Brands: Use of Recalled Attributes and Prior Overall Evaluations

Journal of Consumer Research 15 (2) (September 1988), 169–84.

1991 Association for Consumer Research Best Article Award Winner (as of 1996, the *Journal of Consumer Research* Best Article Award)

Consumers faced choices in which some or all alternatives had to be recalled from memory. Experiments 1 and 2 investigated conditions that lead consumers to use recalled prior evaluations versus recalled brand attribute information as inputs to brand choices. Results suggest that consumers use a potential input to make a choice if it is accessible in memory and if they perceive it as more diagnostic than other accessible potential inputs. The theoretical framework used to interpret these results has the potential to integrate past work on affect referral, the link between memory and judgment, and the role of attitudes in choice.

Martineau, Pierre
Social Classes and Spending Behavior
Journal of Marketing 23 (2) (October 1958), 121–30.
1958 Alpha Kappa Psi Award Winner (as of 1996, the Marketing Science Institute H. Paul Root Award)

While income has generally been the most widely used behavioral indicator in marketing, social-class membership provides a richer dimension of meaning. The individual's consumption patterns actually symbolize his class position, a more significant determinant of his buying behavior than just income. There is a social-class system operative in metropolitan markets which can be isolated and described. The kinds of things a person will or will not buy are strongly related to his class membership, and also whether he is mobile or stable. Likewise the individual's store loyalties and his spend-save aspirations will in considerable part be class related.

McAlister, Leigh
Choosing Multiple Items from a Product Class
Journal of Consumer Research 6 (3) (December 1979), 213–24.
1978 Robert Ferber Award Winner

By focusing on consumer preference for single items, researchers have implicitly assumed that product choices are made independently of each other. For many product classes (e.g., magazines, stereo albums, liquor in a home bar) that assumption is implausible. "Balancing" or "rounding out" a group of items implies dependence among selections. Models incorporating this dependence are constructed and tested.

McCracken, Grant
Culture and Consumption: A Theoretical Account of the Structure and Movement of the Cultural Meaning of Consumer Goods
Journal of Consumer Research 13 (1) (June 1986), 71–84.
1987 Association for Consumer Research Best Article Award Winner (as of 1996, the *Journal of Consumer Research* Best Article Award)

Cultural meaning in a consumer society moves ceaselessly from one location to another. In the usual trajectory, cultural meaning moves first from the culturally constituted world to consumer goods and then from these goods to the individual consumer. Several instruments are responsible for this movement: advertising, the fashion system, and four consumption rituals. This article analyzes the movement of cultural meaning theoretically, showing both where cultural meaning is resident in the contemporary North American consumer system and the means by which this meaning is transferred from one location in this system to another.

Puto, Christopher P.
The Framing of Buying Decisions
Journal of Consumer Research 14 (3) (December 1987), 301–15.
1985 Robert Ferber Award Winner

Research in behavioral decision theory suggests that people use reference points as the basis for judging/comparing the value of decision alternatives, but there has been little research addressing how decision reference points are formed. This paper posits and empirically demonstrates a conceptual framework of the reference point formation process for buying decisions. The basic concepts in the framework are supported, and the resulting reference points are shown to influence choice in a manner consistent with prospect theory.

Rao, Akshay R., and Kent B. Monroe
The Moderating Effects of Prior Knowledge on Cue Utilization in Product Evaluations
Journal of Consumer Research 15 (2) (September 1988), 253–64.
Co-winner of the 1987 Robert Ferber Award

This article examines the dissimilar use of product information cues in product evaluations by differentially familiar subjects. Specifically, the use of price cues and intrinsic product cues for the assessment of product quality is hypothesized to depend on prior knowledge. For a product with a positive quality-price association in the marketplace, the study shows that low-familiar and highly familiar subjects tend to perceive a stronger price-quality relationship than do moderately familiar subjects. Moreover, as subjects' product familiarity increases, the use of intrinsic cues for product quality assessments tends to become relatively stronger.

Richins, Marsha L.
Measuring Emotions in the Consumption Experience
Journal of Consumer Research 24 (2) (September 1997), 127–46.
Co-winner of 2000 Association for Consumer Research Best Article Award Winner (as of 1996, the *Journal of Consumer Research* Best Article Award)

Although consumption-related emotions have been studied with increasing frequency in consumer behavior, issues concerning the appropriate way to measure these emotions remain unresolved. This article reviews the emotion measures currently used in consumer research and the theories on which they are based; it concludes that the existing measures are unsuited for the purpose of measuring consumption-related emotions. The article describes six empirical studies that assess the domain of consumption-related emotions, that identify an appropriate set of consumption emotion descriptors (the CES), and that compare the usefulness of this descriptor set with the usefulness of other measures in assessing consumption-related emotions.

Simonson, Itamar

Choice Based on Reasons: The Case of Attraction and Compromise Effects

Journal of Consumer Research 16 (2) (September 1989), 158–74.

1990 Robert Ferber Award Winner and 1990 Association for Consumer Research Best Article Award Winner (as of 1996, the *Journal of Consumer Research* Best Article Award)

Building on previous research, this article proposes that choice behavior under preference uncertainty may be easier to explain by assuming that consumers select the alternative supported by the best reasons. This approach provides an explanation for the so-called attraction effect and leads to the prediction of a compromise effect. Consistent with the hypotheses, the results indicate that (1) brands tend to gain share when they become compromise alternatives in a choice set; (2) attraction and compromise effects tend to be stronger among subjects who expect to justify their decisions to others; and (3) selections of dominating and compromise brands are associated with more elaborate and difficult decisions.

Simonson, Itamar, and Amos Tversky

Choice in Context: Tradeoff Contrast and Extremeness Aversion

Journal of Marketing Research 29 (3) (August 1992), 281–95.

1997 William F. O'Dell Award Winner

Consumer choice is often influenced by the context, defined by the set of alternatives under consideration. Two hypotheses about the effect of context on choice are proposed. The first hypothesis, tradeoff contrast, states that the tendency to prefer an alternative is enhanced or hindered depending on whether the tradeoffs within the set under consideration are favorable or unfavorable to that option. The second hypothesis, extremeness aversion, states that the attractiveness of an option is enhanced if it is an intermediate option in the choice set and is diminished if it is an extreme option. These hypotheses can explain previous findings (e.g., attraction and compromise effects) and predict some new effects, demonstrated in a series of studies with consumer products as choice alternatives. Theoretical and practical implications of the findings are discussed.

Sirsi, Ajay K., James C. Ward, and Peter H. Reingen

Microcultural Analysis of Variation in Sharing of Causal Reasoning about Behavior

Journal of Consumer Research 22 (4) (March 1996), 345–72.

1996 Robert Ferber Award Winner and 1999 *Journal of Consumer Research* Best Article Award Winner

This article explores the relation of culture to consumption by investigating individual, social, and cultural sources of variation in the sharing of causal reasoning about behavior in two microcultures. The results suggest (1) the importance of intracultural variation in the study of culture, (2) differences between experts and novices as a robust source of this variation, (3) novel insights into the relationship between expertise and sociocultural phenomena, and (4) the potential for investigating attitude structure, categorization, and attribution as products of causal reasoning originating from cultural belief systems. The study also demonstrates the synergy created by diverse research methods.

West, Patricia M.

Predicting Preferences: An Examination of Agent Learning

Journal of Consumer Research 23 (1) (June 1996), 68–80.

1997 Robert Ferber Award Winner

Agent decision making occurs when an individual acts as a purchasing agent for another. Effective agent decision making requires that the agent learn to predict the target's preferences. Two experimental studies demonstrate the impact of providing agents veridical feedback. The results further our understanding of interpersonal prediction and learning from experience. Agents who are given the opportunity to learn from their own successes and failures do not exhibit the false consensus effect, or projection, that has been demonstrated in previous research. Any facilitative effect of similarity in tastes on predictive accuracy disappears when feedback is provided. Information theory is used to establish the informational value of individual instances, as well as an overall distribution of feedback. The results of the studies reported in the present article indicate that agents spend significantly more time considering informative than uninformative feedback, which improves their predictive accuracy.

Additional Relevant Papers: Customer Insight

Anderson, Erin, and Barton Weitz

The Use of Pledges to Build and Sustain Commitment in Distribution Channels

Journal of Marketing Research 29 (1) (February 1992), 18–34. See page 53 for abstract.

2000 Louis W. Stern Award Winner

Bell, David R., and James M. Lattin

Shopping Behavior and Consumer Preference for Store Price Format: Why "Large Basket" Shoppers Prefer EDLP

Marketing Science 17 (1) (Winter 1998), 66–88. See page 115 for abstract.

1999 Frank M. Bass Dissertation Paper Award Winner

Boulding, William, Ajay Kalra, Richard Staelin, and Valarie A. Zeithaml

A Dynamic Process Model of Service Quality: From Expectations to Behavioral Intentions

Journal of Marketing Research 30 (1) (February 1993), 7–27. See page 54 for abstract.

Co-winner of the 1998 William F. O'Dell Award

Braun, Kathryn A.

Postexperience Advertising Effects on Consumer Memory

Journal of Consumer Research 25 (4) (March 1999), 319–34. See page 117 for abstract.

1999 Robert Ferber Award Winner and 2002 *Journal of Consumer Research* Best Article Award Winner

Broniarczyk, Susan M., Wayne D. Hoyer, and Leigh McAlister

Consumers' Perceptions of the Assortment Offered in a Grocery Category: The Impact of Item Reduction

Journal of Marketing Research 35 (2) (May 1998), 166–76. See page 117 for abstract.

2003 William F. O'Dell Award Winner

Burke, Raymond R., and Thomas K. Srull

Competitive Interference and Consumer Memory for Advertising

Journal of Consumer Research 15 (1) (June 1988), 55–68. See page 118 for abstract.

1989 Robert Ferber Award Winner

Carpenter, Gregory S., Rashi Glazer, and Kent Nakamoto

Meaningful Brands from Meaningless Differentiation: The Dependence on Irrelevant Attributes

Journal of Marketing Research 31 (3) (August 1994), 339–50. See page 119 for abstract.

1999 William F. O'Dell Award Winner

Dillon, William R., Thomas J. Madden, Amna Kirmani, and Soumen Mukherjee

Understanding What's in a Brand Rating: A Model for Assessing Brand and Attribute Effects and Their Relationship to Brand Equity

Journal of Marketing Research 38 (4) (November 2001), 415–29. See page 28 for abstract.

2002 Paul E. Green Award Winner

Fournier, Susan

Consumers and Their Brands: Developing Relationship Theory in Consumer Research

Journal of Consumer Research 24 (4) (March 1998), 343–73. See page 29 for abstract.

2001 *Journal of Consumer Research* Best Article Award Winner

Fournier, Susan, and David Glen Mick

Rediscovering Satisfaction

Journal of Marketing 63 (4) (October 1999), 5–23. See page 55 for abstract.

1999 Harold H. Maynard Award Winner

Friestad, Marian, and Peter Wright

The Persuasion Knowledge Model: How People Cope with Persuasion Attempts

Journal of Consumer Research 21 (1) (June 1994), 1–31. See page 120 for abstract.

1997 *Journal of Consumer Research* Best Article Award Winner

Gardner, David M.

Deception in Advertising: A Conceptual Approach

Journal of Marketing 39 (1) (January 1975), 40–6. See page 120 for abstract.

1975 Harold H. Maynard Award Winner

Heide, Jan B.

Interorganizational Governance in Marketing Channels

Journal of Marketing 58 (1) (January 1994), 71–85. See page 56 for abstract.

2001 Louis W. Stern Award Winner

Heilman, Carrie M., Douglas Bowman, and Gordon P. Wright

The Evolution of Brand Preferences and Choice Behaviors of Consumers New to a Market

Journal of Marketing Research 37 (2) (May 2000), 139–55. See page 122 for abstract.

2001 Paul E. Green Award Winner

Keller, Kevin Lane

Conceptualizing, Measuring, and Managing Customer-Based Brand Equity

Journal of Marketing 57 (1) (January 1993), 1–22. See page 30 for abstract.

1993 Harold H. Maynard Award Winner and 2002 Sheth Foundation/*Journal of Marketing* Award Winner

Kivetz, Ran

Promotion Reactance: The Role of Effort-Reward Congruity

Journal of Consumer Research 31 (4) (March 2005), 725–36. See page 123 for abstract.

2005 Robert Ferber Award Winner

Levy, Sidney J.

Interpreting Consumer Mythology: A Structural Approach to Consumer Behavior

Journal of Marketing 45 (3) (Summer 1981), 49–61. See page 97 for abstract.

1981 Harold H. Maynard Award Winner

Mela, Carl F., Sunil Gupta, and Donald R. Lehmann

The Long-Term Impact of Promotion and Advertising on Consumer Brand Choice

Journal of Marketing Research 34 (2) (May 1997), 248–61. See page 41 for abstract.

1998 Paul E. Green Award Winner and 2002 William F. O'Dell Award Winner

Mitra, Anusree, and John G. Lynch, Jr.

Toward a Reconciliation of Market Power and Information Theories of Advertising Effects on Price Elasticity

Journal of Consumer Research 21 (4) (March 1995), 644–59. See page 125 for abstract.

1995 Robert Ferber Award Winner

Moore, Elizabeth S., and Richard J. Lutz

Children, Advertising, and Product Experiences: A Multimethod Inquiry

Journal of Consumer Research 26 (1) (June 2000), 31–48. See page 125 for abstract.

Co-winner of the 2003 *Journal of Consumer Research* Best Article Award

---

Muniz, Albert M, Jr., and Thomas C. O'Guinn

Brand Community

Journal of Consumer Research 27 (4) (March 2001), 412–31. See page 30 for abstract.

2004 *Journal of Consumer Research* Best Article Award Winner

Nordhielm, Christie L.

The Influence of Level of Processing on Advertising Repetition Effects

Journal of Consumer Research 29 (3) (December 2002), 371–82. See page 128 for abstract.

2003 Robert Ferber Award Winner

Nowlis, Stephen M., and Itamar Simonson

The Effect of New Product Features on Brand Choice

Journal of Marketing Research (33) (1) (February 1996), 36–46. See page 18 for abstract.

2001 William F. O'Dell Award Winner

Obermiller, Carl

Varieties of Mere Exposure: The Effects of Processing Style and Repetition on Affective Response

Journal of Consumer Research 12 (1) (June 1985), 17–30. See page 128 for abstract.

1983 Robert Ferber Award Winner

O'Guinn, Thomas C., and L. J. Shrum

The Role of Television in the Construction of Consumer Reality

Journal of Consumer Research 23 (4) (March 1997), 278–94. See page 129 for abstract.

Co-winner of the 2000 *Journal of Consumer Research* Best Article Award

Ritson, Mark, and Richard Elliott

The Social Uses of Advertising: An Ethnographic Study of Adolescent Advertising Audiences

Journal of Consumer Research 26 (3) (December 1999), 260–77. See page 131 for abstract.

2000 Robert Ferber Award Winner

Spreng, Richard A., Scott B. MacKenzie, and Richard W. Olshavsky

A Reexamination of the Determinants of Consumer Satisfaction

Journal of Marketing 60 (3) (July 1996), 15–32. See page 59 for abstract.

Co-winner of the 1996 Harold H. Maynard Award

Stern, Louis W., and Torger Reve

Distribution Channels as Political Economies: A Framework for Comparative Analysis

Journal of Marketing 44 (3) (Summer 1980), 52–64. See page 59 for abstract.

Co-winner of the 1980 Harold H. Maynard Award

Ter Hofstede, Frenkel, Jan-Benedict E. M. Steenkamp, and Michel Wedel

International Market Segmentation Based on Consumer-Product Relations

Journal of Marketing Research 36 (1) (February 1999), 1–17. See page 100 for abstract.

2004 William F. O'Dell Award Winner

van Osselaer, Stijn M. J., and Joseph W. Alba

Consumer Learning and Brand Equity

Journal of Consumer Research 27 (1) (June 2000), 1–16. See page 32 for abstract.

Co-winner of the 2001 Robert Ferber Award

Wells, William D.

Psychographics: A Critical Review

Journal of Marketing Research 12 (2) (May 1975), 196–213. See page 101 for abstract.

1980 William F. O'Dell Award Winner

Zeithaml, Valarie A.

Consumer Response to In-Store Price Information Environments

Journal of Consumer Research 8 (4) (March 1982), 357–69. See page 137 for abstract.

1981 Robert Ferber Award Winner

Zeithaml, Valarie A.

Consumer Perceptions of Price, Quality, and Value: A Means-End Model and Synthesis of Evidence

Journal of Marketing 52 (3) (July 1988), 2–22. See page 137 for abstract.

1988 Harold H. Maynard Award Winner

9

Strategy

This chapter describes award-winning papers on strategy, with an emphasis on the nature of competition. Customers are equally important to marketing strategy, but they are discussed in Chapter 4, "Managing Relationships with Customers and Organizations." Papers in this chapter have been grouped (loosely) under six themes and ordered to highlight how conceptualizations of marketing strategy have evolved over time. Papers in the first group characterize the fundamental elements of a theory of competitive strategy and (ultimately) lead to a comparative advantage theory of competition. In the second group of papers, marketers describe competition in markets for goods, services, and information and describe the different means of acquiring comparative advantage that may emerge (e.g., different bundling strategies).

The next three groups of award-winning papers consider the interplay of different elements of marketing strategy, focusing on new product strategy, pricing strategy, and the structure of channels of distribution. Many of these papers develop analytical models that consider competition under different scenarios and derive long-run equilibrium conditions. In this way, researchers are able to identify profitable strategies (for different parties in a supply chain or network) under somewhat stylized market conditions. Papers in the first of these three groups analyze how the timing of a brand's entry into a product category influences business performance; they show how these analyses have become more sophisticated—and the results more equivocal. Papers in the second and third groups describe pricing strategies and distribution channel structures, respectively.

The sixth group of award-winning papers considers how alliances between firms provide opportunities for competitive advantage. This research dovetails with the research on interorganizational relationships described in Chapter 4.

Foundations of Competitive Strategy

Smith (1956) discussed two key elements of competitive strategy: product differentiation and market segmentation. There is a long-standing notion in marketing of a product life cycle—the notion that products flourish and then decline. In a very early paper, Alexander (1964) presented a plan for gathering information about products, evaluating them, and (if necessary) eliminating them. This notion evolved into a more complex assessment of the product portfolio, with a growing emphasis on identifying a sustainable competitive advantage for a multiproduct, multimarket firm (Day 1977; Wensley 1981).

More generally, Day and Wensley (1988) developed a conceptual framework in which effective strategies are grounded in analyses of competitive position and sources of differential advantage (e.g., skills, resources) that yield superior customer value and cost in the future. They emphasized a balance of customer and competitor perspectives, as well as considering supply-side and demand-side factors. Dickson (1992) developed a theory of competitive rationality, based on economic psychology and information economics, which proposed that a firm's success depends on the imperfect rationality of its marketing planners. These conceptual advances led to changes in the notion of a product life cycle that recognized the competitive processes that accompany the evolution of a market and ultimately influence business performance (Lambkin and Day 1989).

Hunt and Morgan (1995) proposed a comparative advantage theory of competition, suitable for analyzing macro and micro phenomena, and contrasted it with the neoclassical theory of perfect competition. They identified market orientation as a potential resource for comparative advantage. In the past ten years, Hunt and Morgan's theory has heavily influenced research, and their key constructs are embedded in the customer management and metrics research streams.

Comparative Advantage for Firms Selling Goods, Services, and Information

Marketers have been interested in learning how product quality can be used to gain comparative advantage. Kirmani and Rao (2000) discussed how a firm may signal the unobservable quality of its products through different marketing mix variables. Iyer and Soberman (2000) examined value-adding product modifications that may increase customer acquisition or customer retention.

In conceptual papers, researchers have frequently distinguished services and information from conventional goods (tangibles). Lovelock (1983) proposed five schemes for classifying services in ways that transcend industry boundaries; his goal was to gain insight into how the nature of the service influences the marketing task. Glazer (1991) presented a series of propositions that predicted the consequences of increasing information intensity for some key components of firm strategy and organizational structure.

More recently, marketers have begun to analyze competition in information markets. Sarvary and Parker (1997) addressed the question of whether competition is fundamentally different when competing firms sell information rather than traditional goods and services, and if so, why that was true. They concluded that information markets face unique competitive structures because information may be either a complement or a substitute. Hence, consumers are likely to purchase from multiple sellers when the reliability of information is low and the sources are independent; whereas they will treat information products as substitutes and buy from a single source when reliability of information is high. In other words, unreliable information invites a competitor. Subsequently, Chen, Narasimhan, and Zhang (2001) showed how superior knowledge of customers (that improves targetability) can be a comparative advantage.

Strategic bundling of prices and products has become increasingly common; Stremersch and Tellis (2002) have observed that from a conceptual standpoint, different bundling strategies are optimal in different contexts.

The Influence of Market Entry and Timing on Market Share

In understanding the dynamics of evolving markets, a crucial question is how a brand's order of entry into a product category is related to business performance, especially market share. Analyzing a sample of 92 brands across 24 consumer product categories, Urban et al. (1986) showed that order of entry is inversely related to market share—first movers, or pioneers, have an advantage. Their findings were confirmed by predictions on a holdout sample of 47 brands in 12 categories. Entry barriers and switching costs could be responsible for the pioneer advantage observed in both consumer and industrial markets. Operating on that assumption, Hauser and Shugan (1983) showed how a firm might adjust its marketing expenditures and price to defend its product's market position from attack by a competitive new product. Carpenter and Nakamoto (1989), by contrast, argued that it is not entry barriers and switching costs, but rather the way in which consumers form their preferences that confers an advantage on pioneers.

Additional award-winning papers on the topic of market entry and timing (as well as on diffusion of innovation) are summarized in Chapter 1, "New Products, Growth, and Innovation." Those papers suggest that the field is moving toward a richer, more nuanced understanding of the effects of market entry and timing in the short and long run. Recent research has also begun to examine the effect of new product introductions and other marketing variables on shareholder value. Award-winning papers on that topic are summarized in Chapter 3, "Metrics Linking Marketing to Financial Performance."

Pricing Strategy

There is a large stream of research on pricing strategy and tactics in marketing, and this topic is also important in the economic literatures. We have described many award-winning papers on pricing tactics in Chapter 7.

Pricing strategy is typically considered to have a long-run orientation. For example, Horsky and Nelson (1992) addressed the question of how to position and price a new brand when incumbents react to its entry by changing their own prices.

The Structure of Distribution Channels

Analytical models are particularly useful for studying strategy in the context of distribution channels because channel relationships entail long-term commitments that are difficult to study. Purohit (1997) evaluated the profitability of various channel structures for each of the players involved in the sale of durable goods through two channels. In his study, the players were an automobile manufacturer and the manufacturer's two sales channels—a rental agency and a dealer. He found that an overlapping channel structure—that is, one in which rental agencies are encouraged to sell their slightly used rental cars in the consumer market—is the most profitable structure for the manufacturer and the rental agency, but the least profitable for the dealer. He characterized the current distribution structure in the automobile industry as a compromise channel and explained why it may have developed.

Balasubramanian (1998) conducted a strategic analysis of competition between direct marketers and conventional retailers that considered consumer and market characteristics. His analyses showed that traditional retail entry analyses are not relevant when a direct channel has a strong presence. He found (surprisingly) that high market coverage—in which direct marketers provide information to all consumers—may depress profits if the product is not well adapted to the direct channel.

Collaborating to Compete

Interestingly, alliances between firms provide opportunities for competitive advantage. Bucklin and Sengupta (1993) showed that alliances are more effective when power and managerial imbalances are reduced and when projects and partners are carefully selected. Amaldoss et al. (2000) developed an analytic model of how different types of alliances (same-function alliances, parallel development of new products, or cross-functional alliances) and profit-sharing arrangements (equal or proportional) influence the resource commitments of both the parties involved. If the market is large, same-function alliances yield the same predicted investment patterns under either profit-sharing arrangement. However, partners developing new products in parallel commit fewer resources to their alliance—although they commit more when profit sharing is proportional to investments.

Research Priorities

Strategy is not among MSI's 2004–2006 first-tier research priorities. However, the Marketing Excellence and Marketing Productivity communities consider many strategic questions to be second-tier priorities. Grouping these research questions under the themes used in this essay, they include:

Comparative Advantage

- creating and pricing product and service bundles
- creating profitable product portfolios
- differences in marketing's impact on financial metrics for nondurables, durables, and services for long-sales-cycle businesses or at different stages of the life cycle

Market Entry and Timing

- making tradeoffs between investments in mature products and markets and investments in new products and markets

Pricing Strategy

- anticipating and influencing competitors' pricing
- understanding and measuring price sensitivity in business-to-business markets
- optimal pricing over time

Last, the Customer Management community is interested in issues relating to the structure of distribution channels and to collaboration among competitors, such as dealing with a dominant customer and how to deal with solutions sellers as intermediaries.

Abstracts: Strategy

Alexander, R. S.
The Death and Burial of "Sick" Products
Journal of Marketing 28 (2) (April 1964), 1–7.
1964 Alpha Kappa Psi Award Winner (as of 1996, the Marketing Science Institute H. Paul Root Award)

Products, like men, are mortal. They flourish for a time, then decline and die. While the death of a man is catastrophic in the sense that it occurs at a specific point in time, that of a product tends to be an indefinite process that may continue until its last user forgets that it ever existed and so will no longer try to buy it. Professor R. S. Alexander presents a thoughtful and practical plan for selecting products for elimination; gathering information about them; making decisions about them; and, if necessary, removing the doomed products from the line.

Amaldoss, Wilfred, Robert J. Meyer, Jagmohan S. Raju, and Amnon Rapoport
Collaborating to Compete
Marketing Science 19 (2) (Spring 2000), 105–26.
2000 Frank M. Bass Dissertation Paper Award Winner and Co-winner of the 2000 John D. C. Little Award

In collaborating to compete, firms forge different types of strategic alliances: same-function alliances, parallel development of new products, and cross-functional alliances. A major challenge in the management of these alliances is how to control the resource commitment of partners to the collaboration. In this research we examine both theoretically and experimentally how the type of an alliance and the prescribed profit-sharing arrangement affect the resource commitments of partners. We model the interaction within an alliance as a noncooperative variable-sum game, in which each firm invests part of its resources to increase the utility of a new product offering. Different types of alliances are modeled by varying how the resources committed by partners in an alliance determine the utility of the jointly-developed new product. We then model the interalliance competition by nesting two independent intra-alliance games in a supergame in which the groups compete for a market. The partners of the winning alliance share the profits in one of two ways: equally or proportionally to their investments. The Nash equilibrium solutions for the resulting games are examined. In the case of same-function alliances, when the market is large the predicted investment patterns under both profit-sharing rules are comparable. Partners developing new products in parallel, unlike the partners in a same-function alliance, commit fewer resources to their alliance. Further, the profit-sharing arrangement matters in such alliances—partners commit more resources when profits are shared proportionally rather than equally.

We test the predictions of the model in two laboratory experiments. We find that the aggregate behavior of the subjects is accounted for remarkably well by the equilibrium solution. As predicted, profit-sharing arrangement did not affect the investment pattern of subjects in same-function alliances when they were in the high-reward condition. Subjects developing products in parallel invested less than subjects in same-function alliance, irrespective of the reward condition. We notice that theory seems to underpredict investments in low-reward conditions. A plausible explanation for this departure from the normative benchmark is that subjects in the low-reward condition were influenced by altruistic regard for their partners. These experiments also clarify the support for the mixed strategy equilibrium: aggregate behavior conforms to the equilibrium solution, though the behavior of individual subjects varies substantially from the norm. Individual-level analysis suggests that subjects employ mixed strategies, but not as fully as the theory demands. This inertia in choice of strategies is consistent with learning trends observed in the investment pattern. A new analysis of Robertson and Gatignon's (1998) field survey data on the conduct of corporate partners in technology alliances is also consistent with our model of same-function alliances. We extend the model to consider asymmetric distribution of endowments among partners in a same-function alliance. Then we examine the implication of extending the strategy space to include more levels of investment. Finally, we outline an extension of the model to consider cross-functional alliances.

Balasubramanian, Sridhar

Mail versus Mall: A Strategic Analysis of Competition between Direct Marketers and Conventional Retailers

Marketing Science 17 (3) (Summer 1998), 181–95.
1998 John D. C. Little Award Winner

Consumers now purchase several offerings from direct sellers, including catalog and Internet marketers. These direct channels exist in parallel with the conventional retail stores. The availability of multiple channels has significant implications for the performance of consumer markets. The literature in marketing and economics has, however, been dominated by a focus on the conventional retail sector. This paper is an effort toward modeling competition in the multiple-channel environment from a strategic viewpoint. At the outset, a parsimonious model that accommodates the following consumer and market characteristics is introduced. First, the relative attractiveness of retail shopping varies across consumers. Second, the fit with the direct channel varies across product categories. Third, the strength of existing retail presence in local markets moderates competition. Fourth, in contrast with the fixed location of the retail store that anchors its localized market power, the location of the direct marketer is irrelevant to the competitive outcome.

The model is first applied in a setting where consumers have complete knowledge of product availability and prices in all channels. In the resulting equilibrium, the direct marketer acts as a competitive wedge between retail stores. The direct presence is so strong that each retailer competes against the remotely located direct marketer, rather than against neighboring retailers. This outcome has implications for the marketing mix of retailers, which has traditionally been tuned to attract consumers choosing between retail stores. In the context of market entry, conditions under which a direct channel can access a local market in retail entry equilibrium are derived. Our analysis suggests that the traditional focus on retail entry equilibria may not yield informative or relevant findings when direct channels are a strong presence.

Next, the role of information in multiple-channel markets is modeled. This issue is particularly relevant in the context of direct marketing where the seller can typically control the level of information in the marketplace, sometimes on a customer-by-customer basis (e.g., by deciding on the mailing list for a catalog campaign). When a certain fraction of consumers does not receive information from the direct marketer, the retailers compete with each other for that fraction of the market. The retailer's marketing mix has to be tuned, in this case, to jointly address direct and neighboring retail competition. The level of information disseminated by the direct marketer is shown to have strategic implications, and the use of market coverage as a lever to control competition is described. Even with zero information costs, providing information to all consumers may not be optimal under some circumstances. In particular, when the product is not well adapted to the direct channel, the level of market information about the direct option should ideally be lowered. The only way to compete with retailers on a larger scale with a poorly adapted product is by lowering direct prices, which lowers profits. Lowering market information levels and allowing retailers to compete more with each other facilitates a higher equilibrium retail price. In turn, this allows a higher direct price to be charged and improves overall direct profit. On the other hand, when the product is well adapted, increasing direct market presence and engaging in greater competition with the retail sector yields higher returns.

The finding that high market coverage may depress profits raises some issues for further exploration. First, implementing the optimal coverage is straightforward when the seller controls the information mechanism, as in the case of catalog marketing. The Internet, in contrast, is an efficient mechanism to transmit information, but does not provide the sellers with such control over the level of market information. A key reason is that the initiative to gather information on the Internet lies largely with consumers. The design and implementation of mechanisms to control aggregate information levels in electronic markets can, therefore, be an important theme for research and managerial interest. Second, direct marketers have traditionally relied on the statistical analysis of customer records to decide on contact policies. The analysis in this paper reveals that these policies can have significant strategic implications as well. Research that integrates the statistical and strategic aspects could make a valuable contribution. The paper concludes with a discussion of issues for future research in multiple-channel markets, including avenues to model competition in settings with multiple direct marketers.

Bucklin, Louis P., and Sanjit Sengupta
Organizing Successful Co-Marketing Alliances
Journal of Marketing 57 (2) (April 1993), 32–46.
1993 Alpha Kappa Psi Award Winner (as of 1996, the Marketing Science Institute H. Paul Root Award)
An earlier version of this paper appeared as MSI Report No. 92–120, "Balancing Co-Marketing Alliances for Effectiveness."

Co-marketing alliances between firms afford fresh opportunity for strategic advantage. Data from 98 alliances show that gains in effectiveness can be obtained by reducing power and managerial imbalances. Careful project selection and better matching of potential partners also help to enhance alliance effectiveness.

Carpenter, Gregory S., and Kent Nakamoto
Consumer Preference Formation and Pioneering Advantage
Journal of Marketing Research 26 (3) (August 1989), 285–98.
1994 William F. O'Dell Award Winner

Market pioneers outsell later entrants in both consumer and industrial markets. Entry barriers arising from preemptive positioning and switching costs have been advanced to explain this market share difference, termed "pioneering advantage." However, empirical studies show that pioneering advantages are present even in mature markets in which brands reposition and switching costs are minimal. In these cases, the authors argue that pioneering advantage can arise from the process by which consumers learn about brands and form their preferences. This process can produce a preference structure that favors the pioneer, making it difficult for later entrants to "compete away" the pioneer's large market share, even if brands can reposition and switching costs are minimal.

Chen, Yuxin, Chakravarthi Narasimhan, and Z. John Zhang
Individual Marketing with Imperfect Targetability
Marketing Science 20 (1) (Winter 2001), 23–41.
2001 Frank M. Bass Dissertation Paper Award Winner and Co-winner of the 2001 John D. C. Little Award

Our research investigates the competitive ramifications of individual marketing and information management in today's information-intensive marketing environments. The specific managerial issues we address are as follows. First, what kinds of incentive environments do competing firms face when they can only target individual customers imperfectly? Second, does the improvement in an industry's targetability intensify price competition in the industry such that all competing firms become worse off? Third, should a firm share its customer knowledge so as to improve its rival's targetability? Fourth, how should an information vendor sell its information that can improve a firm's targetability? Finally, do competing firms have the same incentives to invest in their own targetability?

To answer those questions, we develop a simple model à la Narasimhan (1988), in which each of the two competing firms have their own loyal customers and compete for common switchers. We assume that each firm can classify its own loyal customers and switchers correctly only with a less-than-perfect probability. This means that each firm's perceived customer segmentation differs from the actual customer segmentation. Based on their perceived reality, these two competing firms engage in price competition. As an extension, we also allow the competing firms to make their investment decisions to acquire targetability. We show that when individual marketing is feasible, but imperfect, improvements in targetability by either or both competing firms can lead to win-win competition for both even if both players behave noncooperatively and the market does not expand. Win-win competition results from the fact that as a firm becomes better at distinguishing its price-insensitive loyal customers from the switchers, it is motivated to charge a higher price to the former. However, due to imperfect targetability, each firm mistakenly perceives some price-sensitive switchers as price-insensitive loyal customers and charges them all a higher price. These misperceptions thus allow its competitors to acquire those mistargeted customers without lowering their prices and, hence, reduce the rival firm's incentive to cut prices. This effect softens price competition in the market and qualitatively changes the incentive environment for competing firms engaged in individual marketing. A "prisoner's dilemma" occurs only when targetability in a market reaches a sufficiently high level.

This win-win perspective on individual marketing has many managerial implications. First, we show that superior knowledge of individual customers can be a competitive advantage. However, this does not mean that a firm should always protect its customer information from its competitors. To the contrary, we find that competing firms can all benefit from exchanging individual customer information with each other at the nascent stage of individual marketing, when firms' targetability is low. Indeed, under certain circumstances, a firm may even find it profitable to give away this information unilaterally. However, as individual marketing matures (as firms' targetability becomes sufficiently high), further improvements in targetability will intensify price competition and lead to prisoner's dilemma. Therefore, it is not only prudent politics but also a business imperative for an industry to seize the initiative on the issue of protecting customer privacy so as to ensure win-win competition in the industry. Second, we show that the firm with a larger number of loyal customers tends to invest more in targetability when the cost of acquiring targetability is high. However, the firm with a smaller loyal base can, through information investment, acquire a higher level of targetability than the firm with a larger loyal base as long as the cost of acquiring targetability is not too high. As the cost further decreases, competing firms will all have more incentives to increase their investments in targetability until they achieve the highest feasible level. Third, an information vendor should make its information available nonexclusively (exclusively) when its information is associated with a low (high) level of targetability. When the vendor does sell its information exclusively, it should target a firm with a small loyal following if it can impart a high level of targetability to that firm. Finally, our analysis shows that an information-intensive environment does not doom small firms. In fact, individual marketing may provide a good opportunity for a small firm to leapfrog a large firm. The key to leapfrogging is a high level of targetability or customer knowledge.

Day, George S.
Diagnosing the Product Portfolio
Journal of Marketing 41 (2) (April 1977), 29–38.
1977 Alpha Kappa Psi Award Winner (as of 1996, the Marketing Science Institute H. Paul Root Award)

How to avoid costly applications of the product portfolio approach resulting from incorrect measurements, unfeasible strategies, and violation of basic assumptions about market share dominance and product life cycle.

Day, George S., and Robin Wensley

Assessing Advantage: A Framework for Diagnosing Competitive Superiority

Journal of Marketing 52 (2) (April 1988), 1–20.

1988 Alpha Kappa Psi Award Winner (as of 1996, the Marketing Science Institute H. Paul Root Award)

Strategy is about seeking new edges in a market while slowing the erosion of present advantages. Effective strategy moves are grounded in valid and insightful monitoring of the current competitive position coupled with evidence that reveals the skills and resources affording the most leverage on future cost and differentiation advantages. Too often the available measures and methods do not satisfy these requirements. Only a limited set of measures may be used, depending on whether the business starts with the market and uses a customer-focused approach or alternatively adopts a competitor-centered perspective. To overcome possible myopia, the evidence of advantage should illuminate the sources of advantage as well as the manifestations of superior customer value and cost superiority, and should be based on a balance of customer and competitor perspectives.

Dickson, Peter Reid

Toward a General Theory of Competitive Rationality

Journal of Marketing 56 (1) (January 1992), 69–83.

1992 Harold H. Maynard Award Winner

The author develops a theory of competitive rationality that proposes a firm's success depends on the imperfect procedural rationality of its marketing planners. Theories of economic psychology and information economics are integrated with the Austrian economic school of thought and with marketing management concepts and scholarship. Implications for managers and scholars are discussed.

Glazer, Rashi

Marketing in an Information-Intensive Environment: Strategic Implications of Knowledge as an Asset

Journal of Marketing 55 (4) (October 1991), 1–19.

1991 Harold H. Maynard Award Winner

The author presents a framework for thinking about the impact of information and information technology on marketing. The focus is on the concept of "information" or "knowledge" as both an asset to be managed and a variable to be researched. After developing a particular operationalization of the value of information in marketing contexts, which can be used to describe firms in terms of their relative levels of "information intensity," the author presents a series of propositions examining the consequences of increasing information intensity for some key components of firm strategy and organizational structure. The concepts discussed are illustrated with a description of the transaction-based information systems that are being implemented in a variety of firms in pursuit of competitive advantage.

Hauser, John R., and Steven M. Shugan
Defensive Marketing Strategies
Marketing Science 2 (4) (Autumn 1983), 319–60.
1983 Best Paper Award Winner (as of 1988, the John D.C. Little Award)

This paper analyzes how a firm should adjust its marketing expenditures and its price to defend its position in an existing market from attack by a competitive new product. Our focus is to provide usable managerial recommendations on the strategy of response. In particular we show that if products can be represented by their position in a multiattribute space, consumers are heterogeneous and maximize utility, and awareness advertising and distribution can be summarized by response functions, then for the profit maximizing firm: (a) it is optimal to decrease awareness advertising, (b) it is optimal to decrease the distribution budget unless the new product can be kept out of the market, (c) a price increase may be optimal, and (d) even under the optimal strategy, profits decrease as a result of the competitive new product. Furthermore, if the consumer tastes are uniformly distributed across the spectrum (a) a price decrease increases defensive profits, (b) it is optimal (at the margin) to improve product quality in the direction of the defending product's strength and (c) it is optimal (at the margin) to reposition by advertising in the same direction. In addition we provide practical procedures to estimate (1) the distribution of consumer tastes and (2) the position of the new product in perceptual space from sales data and knowledge of the percent of consumers who are aware of the new product and find it available. Competitive diagnostics, such as the angle of attack, are introduced to help the defending manager.

Horsky, Dan, and Paul Nelson
New Brand Positioning and Pricing in an Oligopolistic Market
Marketing Science 11 (2) (Spring 1992), 133–53.
1992 Frank M. Bass Dissertation Paper Award Winner and 1992 John D. C. Little Award Winner

The positioning and pricing of a new brand requires knowledge about the relationship of both demand and cost with potential attribute locations and prices. This paper addresses this problem and illustrates it in the context of the automobile market. Multi-attribute expected utility theory which allows for consumer uncertainty about the brands is used to model individuals' behavior. Attribute weights are estimated from market survey data on brands' attributes and preferences using LINMAP as an estimation procedure. Expected utility is then updated using the multinomial logit model and choice data to account for the observation that stated preferences do not perfectly reflect the eventual choice. It is hypothesized that, when faced with an actual choice, price may become more important to the consumer, while other attributes may become more or less important than is reflected in stated preferences. The resulting estimated choice probabilities are aggregated to form demand functions facing each brand which depend on all brands' prices and attribute space locations. Assuming there is a price equilibrium in the existing market and that firms have the same variable cost function, variable costs as a function of a brand's attribute levels are estimated. Given the demand and cost functions facing each firm including the potential new entrant, the profit maximizing positioning and pricing of a new brand is analyzed using a game theoretic approach. A solution is sought under the assumption that incumbents react to entry by changing their prices. Possible approaches to the translation of the perceptual attribute positioning of the new brand to physical and engineering attributes are reviewed. Improvements and future extensions of the study are discussed.

Hunt, Shelby D., and Robert M. Morgan
The Comparative Advantage Theory of Competition
Journal of Marketing 59 (2) (April 1995), 1–15.
1995 Harold H. Maynard Award Winner and 2004 Sheth Foundation/*Journal of Marketing* Award

A new theory of competition is evolving in the strategy literature. The authors explicate the foundations of this new theory, the "comparative advantage theory of competition," and contrast them with the neoclassical theory of perfect competition. They argue that the new theory of competition explains key macro and micro phenomena better than neoclassical perfect competition theory. Finally, they further explicate the theory of comparative advantage by evaluating a market orientation as a potential resource for comparative advantage.

Iyer, Ganesh, and David Soberman
Markets for Product Modification Information
Marketing Science 19 (3) (Summer 2000), 203–25.
Co-winner of the 2000 John D. C. Little Award

An important product strategy for firms in mature markets is value-adding modifications to existing products. Marketing information that reveals consumers' preferences, buying habits, and lifestyle is critical for the identification of such product modifications. We consider two types of value-adding modifications that are often facilitated by marketing information: retention-type modifications that increase the attractiveness of a product to a firm's loyal customers, and conquesting-type modifications that allow a firm to increase the appeal of its product to a competitor's loyal customers. We examine two aspects of the markets for product modification information: (1) the manner in which retention and conquesting modifications affect competition between downstream firms, and (2) the optimal selling and pricing policies for a vendor who markets product modification information. We consider several aspects of the vendor's contracting problem, including how a vendor should package and target the information to the downstream firms and whether the vendor should limit the type of information that is sold. This research also examines when a vendor can gain by offering exclusivity to a firm.

We address these issues in a model consisting of an information vendor facing two downstream firms that sell differentiated products. The model analyzes how information contracting is affected by differentiation in the downstream market and the quality of the information (in terms of how "impactful" the resulting modifications are). We analyze two possible scenarios. In the first, the information facilitates modifications that increase the appeal of products to the loyal customers of only one of the two downstream firms (i.e., one-sided information). In the second scenario, the information facilitates modifications that are attractive to the loyal consumers of both the firms (i.e., two-sided information). The effect of modifications on downstream competition depends on whether they are of the retention or the conquesting type. A retention-type modification increases the "effective" differentiation between the firms and softens price competition. Conquesting modifications, however, have benefits as well as associated costs. A conquesting modification of low impact reduces the "effective" differentiation between competing products and leads to increased price competition. However, when conquesting modifications are of sufficiently high impact, they also have the benefit of helping a firm to capture the customers of the competitor.

The vendor's strategy for one-sided information always involves selling to one firm, the firm for which the modifications are of the retention type. When the identified modifications are of low impact, this result is expected because conquesting modifications are profit-reducing for downstream firms. However, even when the information identifies high-impact modifications (and positive profits are generated by selling the information as conquesting information), the vendor is strictly better off by targeting his information to the firm for which the modification is the retention type. With two-sided information, the equilibrium strategy is for the vendor to sell the complete packet of information (information on both retention and conquesting modifications) to both downstream firms. However, in equilibrium, both firms only implement retention-type modifications. The information on conquesting modifications is "passive" in the sense that it is never used by downstream firms. Yet the vendor makes strictly greater profit by including it in the packet. This obtains because the price charged for information depends critically on the situation an individual firm encounters by not buying the information. The presence of conquesting information in the packet puts a nonbuyer in a worse situation, and this underlines the "passive power of information." The vendor gains by including the conquesting information even though it is not used in equilibrium.

Kirmani, Amna, and Akshay R. Rao

No Pain, No Gain: A Critical Review of the Literature on Signaling Unobservable Product Quality
Journal of Marketing 64 (2) (April 2000), 66–79.
Co-winner of the 2000 Harold H. Maynard Award

Recent research in information economics has focused on signals as mechanisms to solve problems that arise under asymmetric information. A firm or individual credibly communicates the level of some unobservable element in a transaction by providing an observable signal. When applied to conveying product quality information, this issue is of particular interest to the discipline of marketing. In this article, the authors focus on the ways a firm may signal the unobservable quality of its products through several marketing-mix variables. The authors develop a typology that classifies signals and discuss the available empirical evidence on the signaling properties of several marketing variables. They consider managerial implications of signaling and outline an agenda for future empirical research.

Lambkin, Mary, and George S. Day

Evolutionary Processes in Competitive Markets: Beyond the Product Life Cycle
Journal of Marketing 53 (3) (July 1989), 4–20.
1989 Harold H. Maynard Award Winner

The traditional product life cycle framework has little to say about the competitive processes that accompany the evolution of a market. The first part of the article identifies the major shortcomings of the product life cycle. This analysis is used to establish the requirements for a more comprehensive model that incorporates both demand- and supply-side factors. The second part shows how concepts from population ecology theory can be adapted to satisfy these requirements. With this dynamic theory, specific propositions can be made about changes in competitive structure and performance as the market evolves.

Lovelock, Christopher H.

Classifying Services to Gain Strategic Marketing Insights

Journal of Marketing 47 (3) (Summer 1983), 9–20.

1983 Alpha Kappa Psi Award Winner (as of 1996, the Marketing Science Institute H. Paul Root Award)

The diversity of the service sector makes it difficult to come up with managerially useful generalizations concerning marketing practice in service organizations. This article argues for a focus on specific categories of services and proposes five schemes for classifying services in ways that transcend narrow industry boundaries. In each instance insights are offered into how the nature of the service might affect the marketing task.

Purohit, Devavrat

Dual Distribution Channels: The Competition between Rental Agencies and Dealers

Marketing Science 16 (3) (Summer 1997), 228–45.

Co-winner of the 1997 John D. C. Little Award

Managerial decisions involving marketing channels are among the most critical that an organization must make. Part of the reason for this importance is that relationships between manufacturers and their intermediaries usually involve long-term commitments that are difficult to change. On the other hand, in order to respond to the realities of the marketplace, an organization must be ready to adapt its distribution practices—sometimes under considerable uncertainty about the long-term consequences. Such a problem faces the U.S. automobile industry, which has led manufacturers to experiment with various channel structures. When manufacturers first changed their distribution policies, they were clear about the short-term effect on sales, but were unsure about its longer term impact on profitability. In this article, we develop a model to analyze the marketing of durable products through multiple channels. Our analysis suggests that, even though it was not apparent at the time, manufacturers were indeed behaving optimally when they changed their policies. Our model provides insights not only to automobile manufacturers but also to practitioners and academics who are interested in understanding the unique problems associated with marketing durable products through multiple channels.

We develop a two-period model by assuming that a single manufacturer markets a durable product through two retailers—a rental agency and a dealer. The rental agency focuses mainly on renting the product in a daily rental market while the dealer focuses on selling the product to a different set of customers in the sales market. To model the development of channels in the U.S. automobile industry, we analyze three different channel structures. The first structure, a separate channel, reflects the state of the industry through most of the 1980s, when rental agencies were franchised solely to rent and dealers solely to sell the cars. In response to a decrease in overall sales, manufacturers encouraged rental agencies to sell their "slightly used" rental cars in the consumer market, resulting in the second structure, an overlapping channel. Dealers did not like this arrangement, however, and in the next experiment, a buyback channel, some manufacturers began buying back used rental cars and selling them through dealers.

In terms of the consumer side of the model, we assume that consumers are heterogeneous and have product valuations that are distributed uniformly between a low and a high value. In addition, they recognize that as the durable depreciates with use, its secondhand market value decreases. While both sold and rented goods depreciate with use, we assume, based on an analysis of market prices, that sold goods depreciate at a higher rate than rented goods. Given these different depreciation rates and consumers' underlying utility functions, we develop the market demand functions in the dealer's and rental agency's markets. Then for each of the channel structures, we solve the intermediaries' and manufacturer's problems. The main contribution of this article is that it allows us to evaluate the profitability associated with various channel structures for all the players in our analysis—the dealer, the rental agency, and the manufacturer. In terms of the intermediaries, we find that the overlapping channel is the most profitable structure for the rental agency; on the other hand, it is the least profitable for the dealer. In terms of manufacturer profitability, our model suggests that the separate channel is the least profitable, and the overlapping channel is the most profitable. It is interesting to note that the distribution structure in existence today is more akin to a buyback channel. This strikes us as a compromise channel, which alleviates dealer concerns with the overlapping channel, and yet does not harm rental agencies as much as a separate channel. These are surprising results because conventional wisdom has been that the overlapping channel was competing away profits for all players. This suggests to us that automobile manufacturers were indeed on the right track when they began experimenting with the structure of their distribution channels.

Sarvary, Miklos, and Philip M. Parker

Marketing Information: A Competitive Analysis

Marketing Science 16 (1) (Winter 1997), 24–38.

Co-winner of the 1997 Frank M. Bass Dissertation Paper Award and Co-winner of the 1997 John D. C. Little Award

Selling information that is later used in decision making constitutes an increasingly important business in modern economies (Jensen 1991). Information is sold under a large variety of forms: industry reports, consulting services, database access, and/or professional opinions given by medical, engineering, accounting/financial, and legal professionals, among others. This paper is the first attempt in marketing to study competition in the rapidly emerging information sector. Specifically, we are interested in answering the following questions: (1) Is competition fundamentally different when competing firms sell information rather than traditional goods and services, and—if yes— why? (2) What are the implications of such differences for decision makers (marketers and regulators)? (3) Can we explain some of the observed marketing strategies in the information industry? As such, the audience of the paper includes academics as well as professionals who are interested in understanding what is specific about competition in information markets. Familiarity with the practical implications of such differences and understanding of the mechanisms that drive them is essential for those who are faced with the problem of marketing information.

To answer the above research questions we build a simple game-theoretic model that consists of two firms selling information to a population of consumers who are heterogeneous in their willingness to pay for the quality of information. The most important features of the model are the following. Information products sold by the two firms are modeled as random draws from two normal distributions having equal mean. The variances of these distributions and their correlatedness constitute the product-attribute space, which is assumed to be common knowledge. Consumers are interested in assessing the mean of the distributions and to do so they can buy the sample from any of the firms or they can buy both samples and combine them to obtain a more accurate estimate. Quality of information is linked to the accuracy of consumers' estimate of the mean which in turn is influenced by the accuracy of each sample as well as by their correlatedness. Consumers' utility depends on the quality of information they purchased, on their inherent utility for quality (taste), and on the total price they paid to acquire information. Knowing consumer preferences, firms simultaneously price their information products.

The main finding of the paper is that information markets face unique competitive structures. In particular, the qualitative nature of competition changes depending on basic product characteristics. While traditional products and services compete either as substitutes or as complements in the relevant product-attribute space, information may be one or the other, depending on its position within the same product-attribute space. Said differently, the nature of competition changes qualitatively with a continuous change in basic product-attribute levels. The intuition behind this finding is the following. When purchasing information, consumers facing important decisions may find it beneficial to purchase from several information sellers. This is more likely to happen when the reliability of information is low and the sources of information are independent. Under such conditions information products tend to be complements and, as a result, competition between sellers is relatively mild. In the opposite case, when information is reliable and/or sellers' sources are highly correlated, consumers are satisfied after consulting a single source. In this case, information products are substitutes and sellers tend to undercut one another's prices to induce consumers to choose their brand.

Understanding this discontinuity in competitive structures has important implications for decision makers as very different strategies are optimal under different product characteristics. Under substitution, traditional strategies to avoid competition (e.g., differentiation) are recommended. When the competing products' reliability is generally low (they are complements) firms are better off accommodating competition. In fact, we find that a firm may benefit from "inviting" a competitor. Finally, our findings are also important for regulators of information markets. As the literature on complementarity suggests, price fixing agreements between firms offering complementary products may benefit firms as well as consumers.

Smith, Wendell R.
Product Differentiation and Market Segmentation as Alternative Marketing Strategies
Journal of Marketing 21 (1) (July 1956), 3–8.
1956 Alpha Kappa Psi Award Winner (as of 1996, the Marketing Science Institute H. Paul Root Award)

This article reviews major marketing strategy alternatives that are available to planners and merchandisers of products in an environment characterized by imperfect competition. Under present-day conditions of imperfect competition, marketing managers are generally responsible for selecting the over-all marketing strategy or combination of strategies best suited to a firm's requirements at any particular point in time. The strategy selected may consist of a program designed to bring about the convergence of individual market demands for a variety of products upon a single or limited offering to the market. This is often accomplished by the achievement of product differentiation through advertising and promotion. In this way, variations in the demands of individual consumers are minimized or brought into line by means of effective use of appealing product claims designed to make a satisfactory volume of demand converge upon the product or product line being promoted. In some cases, however, the marketer may determine that it is better to accept divergent demand as a market characteristic and to adjust product lines and marketing strategy accordingly.

Stremersch, Stefan, and Gerard J. Tellis

Strategic Bundling of Products and Prices: A New Synthesis for Marketing

Journal of Marketing 66 (1) (January 2002), 55–72.
2002 Harold H. Maynard Award Winner

Bundling is pervasive in today's markets. However, the bundling literature contains inconsistencies in the use of terms and ambiguity about basic principles underlying the phenomenon. The literature also lacks an encompassing classification of the various strategies, clear rules to evaluate the legality of each strategy, and a unifying framework to indicate when each is optimal. Based on a review of the marketing, economics, and law literature, this article develops a new synthesis of the field of bundling, which provides three important benefits. First, the article clearly and consistently defines bundling terms and identifies two key dimensions that enable a comprehensive classification of bundling strategies. Second, it formulates clear rules for evaluating the legality of each of these strategies. Third, it proposes a framework of 12 propositions that suggest which bundling strategy is optimal in various contexts. The synthesis provides managers with a framework with which to understand and choose bundling strategies. It also provides researchers with promising avenues for further research.

Urban, Glen L., Theresa Carter, Steven Gaskin, and Zofia Mucha

Market Share Rewards to Pioneering Brands: An Empirical Analysis and Strategic Implications

Management Science 32 (6) (June 1986), 645–59.
1986 Best Paper Award Winner (as of 1988, the John D.C. Little Award)

An empirical analysis indicates that the order of entry of a brand into a consumer product category is inversely related to its market share. Market share is modeled as a log linear function of order of entry, time between entries, advertising, and positioning effectiveness. The coefficients of the entry, advertising, and positioning variables are significant in a regression analysis on an initial sample of 82 brands across 24 categories. These findings are confirmed by predictions on 47 not previously analyzed brands in 12 categories. Managerial implications for pioneers and later entrants are identified.

Wensley, Robin

Strategic Marketing: Betas, Boxes, or Basics

Journal of Marketing 45 (3) (Summer 1981), 173–82.

Co-winner of the 1981 Alpha Kappa Psi Award (as of 1996, the Marketing Science Institute H. Paul Root Award)

This paper is critical of both the financial and marketing approaches to resource allocation problems within the multiproduct, multimarket firm. It is suggested that the financial approach is helpful on the issue of shareholder risk but that the marketing strategy approaches, using box classifications, are ill defined and based on dubious empirical assumptions. Neither approach is the key to identifying sustainable competitive advantage. More emphasis is required on project based assessment of such factors as imitability, flexibility, and positional advantages, as well as specific cost effects.

Additional Relevant Papers: Strategy

Alba, Joseph, John Lynch, Barton Weitz, Chris Janiszewski, Richard Lutz, Alan Sawyer, and Stacy Wood

Interactive Home Shopping: Consumer, Retailer, and Manufacturer Incentives to Participate in Electronic Marketplaces

Journal of Marketing 61 (3) (July 1997), 38–53. See page 53 for abstract.

1997 Marketing Science Institute H. Paul Root Award Winner and 2005 Louis W. Stern Award Winner

Assunção, João L., and Robert J. Meyer

The Rational Effect of Price Promotions on Sales and Consumption

Management Science 39 (5) (May 1993), 517–35. See page 113 for abstract.

1993 Frank M. Bass Dissertation Paper Award Winner

Bakos, Yannis, and Erik Brynjolfsson

Bundling Information Goods: Pricing, Profits, and Efficiency

Management Science 45 (12) (December 1999), 1613–30. See page 113 for abstract.

1999 John D. C. Little Award Winner

Bell, David R., and James M. Lattin

Shopping Behavior and Consumer Preference for Store Price Format: Why "Large Basket" Shoppers Prefer EDLP

Marketing Science 17 (1) (Winter 1998), 66–88. See page 115 for abstract.

1999 Frank M. Bass Dissertation Paper Award Winner

Blattberg, Robert C., and Kenneth J. Wisniewski

Price-Induced Patterns of Competition

Marketing Science 8 (4) (Autumn 1989), 291–309. See page 116 for abstract.

1989 John D. C. Little Award Winner

Bultez, Alain, and Philippe Naert

S.H.A.R.P.: Shelf Allocation for Retailers' Profit

Marketing Science 7 (3) (Summer 1988), 211–31. See page 118 for abstract.

Co-winner of the 1988 John D. C. Little Award

Clarke, Darral G.

Econometric Measurement of the Duration of Advertising Effect on Sales

Journal of Marketing Research 13 (4) (November 1976), 345–57. See page 119 for abstract.

Co-winner of the 1981 William F. O'Dell Award

Cooper, Lee G.

Strategic Marketing Planning for Radically New Products

Journal of Marketing 64 (1) (January 2000), 1–16. See page 14 for abstract.

2000 Marketing Science Institute H. Paul Root Award Winner

Desiraju, Ramarao, and Steven M. Shugan

Strategic Service Pricing and Yield Management

Journal of Marketing 63 (1) (January 1999), 44–56. See page 120 for abstract.

Co-winner of the 1999 Marketing Science Institute H. Paul Root Award

Givon, Moshe, and Dan Horsky

Untangling the Effects of Purchase Reinforcement and Advertising Carryover

Marketing Science 9 (2) (Spring 1990), 171–87. See page 121 for abstract.

1990 John D. C. Little Award Winner

Golder, Peter N., and Gerard J. Tellis

Pioneer Advantage: Marketing Logic or Marketing Legend?

Journal of Marketing Research 30 (2) (May 1993), 158–70. See page 14 for abstract.
Co-winner of the 1998 William F. O'Dell Award

Golder, Peter N., and Gerard J. Tellis

Will It Ever Fly? Modeling the Takeoff of Really New Consumer Durables

Marketing Science 16 (3) (Summer 1997), 256–70. See page 15 for abstract.
Co-winner of the 1997 Frank M. Bass Dissertation Paper Award

Hoch, Stephen J., Xavier Drèze, and Mary E. Purk

EDLP, Hi-Lo, and Margin Arithmetic

Journal of Marketing 58 (4) (October 1994), 16–27. See page 122 for abstract.
1994 Alpha Kappa Psi Award Winner (as of 1996, the Marketing Science Institute H. Paul Root Award)

Jacobson, Robert, and David A. Aaker

Is Market Share All That It's Cracked Up to Be?

Journal of Marketing 49 (4) (Fall 1985), 11–22. See page 40 for abstract.
1985 Alpha Kappa Psi Award Winner (as of 1996, the Marketing Science Institute H. Paul Root Award)

Jacobson, Robert, and David A. Aaker

The Strategic Role of Product Quality

Journal of Marketing 51 (4) (October 1987), 31–44. See page 123 for abstract.
1987 Alpha Kappa Psi Award Winner (as of 1996, the Marketing Science Institute H. Paul Root Award)

Lodish, Leonard M., Magid Abraham, Stuart Kalmenson, Jeanne Livelsberger, Beth Lubetkin, Bruce Richardson, and Mary Ellen Stevens

How T.V. Advertising Works: A Meta-Analysis of 389 Real World Split Cable T.V. Advertising Experiments

Journal of Marketing Research 32 (2) (May 1995), 125–39. See page 124 for abstract.
2000 William F. O'Dell Award Winner and 1996 Paul E. Green Award Winner

Lusch, Robert F., and James R. Brown

Interdependency, Contracting, and Relational Behavior in Marketing Channels

Journal of Marketing 60 (4) (October 1996), 19–38. See page 56 for abstract.

Co-winner of the 1996 Harold H. Maynard Award and 2002 Louis W. Stern Award Winner

Mohr, Jakki J., Robert J. Fisher, and John R. Nevin

Collaborative Communication in Interfirm Relationships: Moderating Effects of Integration and Control

Journal of Marketing 60 (3) (July 1996), 103–15. See page 57 for abstract.

2003 Louis W. Stern Award Winner

Naik, Prasad A., Murali K. Mantrala, and Alan G. Sawyer

Planning Media Schedules in the Presence of Dynamic Advertising Quality

Marketing Science 17 (3) (Summer 1998), 214–35. See page 126 for abstract.

1998 Frank M. Bass Dissertation Paper Award Winner

Norton, John A., and Frank M. Bass

A Diffusion Theory Model of Adoption and Substitution for Successive Generations of High-Technology Products

Management Science 33 (9) (September 1987), 1069–86. See page 17 for abstract.

1987 Best Paper Award Winner (as of 1988, the John D.C. Little Award)

Ofek, Elie, and Miklos Sarvary

R&D, Marketing, and the Success of Next-Generation Products

Marketing Science 22 (3) (Summer 2003), 355–70. See page 18 for abstract.

Co-winner of the 2003 John D. C. Little Award and the 2004 Frank M. Bass Dissertation Paper Award

Park, C. Whan, Bernard J. Jaworski, and Deborah J. MacInnis

Strategic Brand Concept-Image Management

Journal of Marketing 50 (4) (October 1986), 135–45. See page 31 for abstract.

1986 Alpha Kappa Psi Award Winner (as of 1996, the Marketing Science Institute H. Paul Root Award)

Raju, Jagmohan S., V. Srinivasan, and Rajiv Lal

The Effects of Brand Loyalty on Competitive Price Promotional Strategies

Management Science 36 (3) (March 1990), 276–304. See page 130 for abstract.

1991 Frank M. Bass Dissertation Paper Award Winner

Robertson, Thomas S., and Hubert Gatignon

Competitive Effects on Technology Diffusion

Journal of Marketing 50 (3) (July 1986), 1–12. See page 19 for abstract.

1986 Harold H. Maynard Award Winner

Shankar, Venkatesh, Gregory S. Carpenter, and Lakshman Krishnamurthi

Late Mover Advantage: How Innovative Late Entrants Outsell Pioneers

Journal of Marketing Research 35 (1) (February 1998), 54–70. See page 19 for abstract.

1999 Paul E. Green Award Winner

Sudhir, K.

Structural Analysis of Manufacturer Pricing in the Presence of a Strategic Retailer

Marketing Science 20 (3) (Summer 2001), 244–64. See page 132 for abstract.

2004 Frank M. Bass Dissertation Paper Award Winner

Xie, Jinhong, and Steven M. Shugan

Electronic Tickets, Smart Cards, and Online Prepayments: When and How to Advance Sell

Marketing Science 20 (3) (Summer 2001), 219–43. See page 135 for abstract.

Co-winner of the 2001 John D. C. Little Award

Index of Abstracts by Author(s)